TRUE CRIME STORIES

TRUE CRIME STORIES

Terry Deary

Hippo

Scholastic Children's Books,
Scholastic Publications Ltd,
7-9 Pratt Street, London NW1 OAE, UK

Scholastic Inc.,
555 Broadway, New York, NY 10012-3999, USA

Scholastic Canada Ltd,
123 Newkirk Road, Richmond Hill,
Ontario, Canada L4C 3G5

Ashton Scholastic Pty Ltd,
P O Box 579, Gosford, New South Wales,
Australia

Ashton Scholastic Ltd,
Private Bag 92801, Penrose, Auckland,
New Zealand

First published by Scholastic Publications Ltd, 1994

Text copyright © Terry Deary, 1994
Illustrations copyright © David Wyatt, 1994

ISBN 0 590 55526 X

Typeset by Contour Typesetters, Southall, London
Printed by Cox & Wyman Ltd, Reading, Berks

·C·O·N·T·E·N·T·S·

INTRODUCTION

Crime stories can be exciting. They have all the ingredients that make for an interesting read – danger and suspense, surprise and lots of action.

But in real life crime isn't glamorous and exciting. Criminals aren't heroes – they're sad people who need help. And they leave other people even sadder – the victims and the victims' friends and family.

There will always be crime because there will always be greedy and uncaring people. Luckily there are many, many more people who stick to the laws and get their thrills from crime by reading about it in books. There will always be true crime stories – in the newspapers, on television, in films and in books like this, where you can spend many interesting hours in the company of crime – with none of the risks and the heartaches of being caught.

OUTLaws
The
Glenrowan Ambush

Outlaws are often remembered with affection rather than fear. Their brutal crimes are forgotten and their exciting way of life is remembered . . .

Glenrowan Town, Australia, 1880

Ann Jones polished a glass and placed it behind the bar of the Glenrowan Inn. It was a hot day and getting hotter.

A man struggled through the door of the hotel with a large suitcase. He let it fall to the floor with a clatter. "Excuse *me!*" Ann Jones snapped. "I have just polished that floor!"

The man wiped sweat and dust from his face with a large kerchief. He glared at her from under thick, dark eyebrows. "No. Excuse *me*, lady. Give me a glass of beer."

The landlady squinted at the man suspiciously. His clothes were rough and dirty. He hadn't shaved for several days, and she didn't like the expression on his sullen face. "Can you pay?" she said shortly.

The man sighed and slowly reached for a gun at his belt. He raised it towards her, pulled back the hammer and said menacingly, "I said, give me a glass of beer."

Mrs Jones's small mouth set in a hard line. "Who do you think you are? Ned Kelly?"

The man pushed the gun back into its holster and walked towards her. He rested two huge hands on the bar and leaned forward. "You recognise me from the Wanted posters, then?" he asked.

The woman swallowed hard. "You *are* Ned Kelly?"

The man managed a small smile. "That's right. And Ned Kelly doesn't pay for his beer. Make that four beers. The boys'll be along in a minute."

The front door of the hotel swung open and a group of people shuffled in. They were silent and afraid. Children clung to their mothers and babies whimpered tiredly. When the bar room was filled the rest of Kelly's gang strolled in holding pistols and rifles.

Kelly swigged at his beer. "Mind that case by the door!" he shouted as one of his men stumbled.

"Sorry, Ned," the man said.

"Now, listen here!" the outlaw called. A hundred pairs of dismayed eyes turned towards him. "If you don't give us any trouble then you won't be harmed. Understand?" There was a murmur of agreement from the adults. "Now, make yourselves comfortable. I expect we'll be here some time!"

Some of the hostages settled on chairs and others sat on the floor. Mrs Jones did her best to give them all some drinks and a little food, then returned to the bar.

"What do you hope to gain from this, Mr Kelly? These people haven't done you any harm!" she argued.

He gave her a hard stare. "And have *I* done *them* any harm?"

"You threatened them. You've brought them here against their will! Don't you realise the police will be here on the next train? It's due in a couple of hours!"

Kelly grinned. "Hear that, Dan?" he called to his brother. "The police will be here in two hours on the train! And what will happen when the police get here?"

"Hah! The train will be derailed. Joe Bryne's arranging it now!"

Kelly nodded. "So, you see. We'll finish off those that the train wreck doesn't kill! We don't want these good people of Glenrowan to suffer. It's the *police* we're after. You're just the bait – Glenrowan is the trap!"

The sun beat down on the tin roof of the hotel. The gang drank. Kelly went and sat on his precious case. The more he drank the more talkative he became. "You lot should hate the police as much as I do! My old pa was sent to Australia as a convict. All he did was steal a few pigs! Is that fair?"

He pointed at a small man in a dark suit. It was Andrew Wilson, the local schoolmaster. "No, Mr Kelly," he said.

"It killed my old pa. Then the state troopers started picking on my family, didn't they? Wanted to put us in jail for the smallest thing. Couldn't get an honest job, could I? Had to take to horse-thieving, didn't I?"

"Yes, Mr Kelly!"

"Sent Ma to jail for three years for hitting Constable Fitzpatrick – when he was pointing a gun at her! Was that fair? And me and Dan had to go out in the bush to hide. We tried to make an honest living – looking for gold, making liquor – but they came after us. Had to kill them, didn't we?"

"Yes, Mr Kelly!"

"And they put a price on our heads. One thousand pounds! We couldn't go back after that, could we?"

"Had to take to robbing banks," Dan Kelly put in.

"Robbing banks," Ned Kelly nodded.

"And killing," Mrs Jones said boldly.

"No!" Kelly shouted. "We never harmed a soul – never fired a shot. You are our friends!" he cried. "The police are out to get you too. The police and the British. You've got to fight them!" he told the schoolmaster.

"I'm not very good at fighting, Mr Kelly," the little man replied.

"That's why you need us to do your fighting for you," Kelly said. "You should be supporting us."

"Oh, but I do, Mr Kelly," the man agreed nervously.

"Then keep a watch on that door while Steve Hart goes to see where that train's got to," Kelly said.

Hart rose, stretched and lumbered out of the door. The hot afternoon air gushed in. The little school teacher moved towards the door. Mrs Jones gave him a signal with her eyes as if to say, "Escape now."

The schoolmaster turned pale and looked back at Kelly. Mrs Jones picked up a brandy bottle. "Here, Mr Kelly, try something a little stronger. That train's often late getting in."

Kelly took the bottle, drank deeply from it and passed it to his brother. With the heat and the strong drink the two men were soon nodding drowsily in their seats.

The schoolmaster rose on trembling legs. The townspeople watched silently as he moved towards the door. Glaring sunlight flared for a moment as the door swung open. Ned Kelly grunted and looked up. But the teacher was gone and the room silent apart from Dan's snoring.

It was after midnight when the front door of the hotel clattered open and Bryne and Hart tumbled in. "Ned!" Bryne cried, shaking the outlaw awake. "It didn't work . . . the train wasn't derailed. Someone must have warned them. The police are on their way. Dozens of them!"

Kelly shook his head to clear it. "Get the people out of here. We're going to have to fight this one out. We've done it before, we'll do it again."

As Mrs Jones hustled the frightened adults and sleepy children out of the back door of the hotel, the outlaws prepared their guns and ammunition.

"We've never faced odds like this before, Ned," Bryne whined.

Kelly laughed and slapped the case he was sitting on. "And the police have never faced this before," he snorted.

Ann Jones knew she should have joined the others in their flight, but something held her there. She just had to know what was in that case – perhaps some new kind of gun. It was certainly metal, she guessed, from the way it rattled.

Kelly tore at the straps and pieces of steel tumbled onto the floor. A voice cried from the darkness outside, "We've got the place surrounded, Kelly! Come out with your hands up!"

The outlaw leader swore loudly, using words Mrs Jones had never heard before. Her eyes widened in surprise as Kelly picked up the pieces of steel and began to assemble them. She knew she had to get out to warn the police of Kelly's surprise. She also knew that the police could well shoot her as soon as she stepped outside the door.

She picked up her drying cloth. The outlaws were crouched by the dark rectangles of window. The lamps had been blown out. Creeping towards the back door, she stretched out a hand timidly and waved the white cloth.

There was no gunfire to snatch the cloth from her hand as she edged forward on hands and knees. A voice called softly from the shadows, "It's all right, Mrs Jones: it's safe! But hurry!" The landlady stumbled to her feet and ran into the arms of her rescuer. The nervous little man wrapped his arms around her and held her tightly as he led her to the safety of the livery stable at the back of the hotel.

"Why, Andrew Wilson," she blushed. "No one's held me like that since my husband died."

The little schoolmaster smiled. "They should, Mrs Jones. You're a very brave woman."

"And you're a very brave man – though you don't look it," she replied. "Now help me find the officer in charge. I've something very important to tell him about that Kelly ... it's a matter of life and death!"

Shots were fired at the hotel throughout the night. It kept the outlaws on edge. When daylight came the police would close in. They could wait for weeks until the men were starved into giving up.

They didn't have to wait for weeks.

As the morning sun began to chase the shadows from the

dusty street the front door of the Glenrowan Inn opened. The police were ready for Kelly – Mrs Jones had warned them – but they were still stunned by what they saw. The outlaw was covered from his head to his thighs in armour – home-made, crudely put together, but bullet-proof and fearsome to see.

From inside the metal tube of a helmet came Kelly's voice. "Fire away! You can't hurt me!"

He began blasting at the police as they cowered in their hiding places. Kelly was an excellent shot but the armour made him clumsy and the slit in the helmet gave him a poor sight of the enemy. Cautiously the police raised their heads and their rifles. Bullets rattled off Kelly's armour and made him stagger, but he still came forward. Joe Bryne tried to shelter behind his leader but the rain of bullets brought him to the ground.

Ann Jones and Andrew Wilson watched from the windows of the school building. "I told them . . . why don't they do what I told them?" she moaned. Then an officer rushed out into the street with a shotgun, aimed quickly at Kelly's legs and fired.

"*That's* what I told them!" the widow cried gleefully as the outlaw crashed to the ground and the police rushed forward to arrest him.

Australia's most wanted man had gone down fighting.

Outlaws – FACT FILE

Outlaws are better remembered than the men who hunted them down, or the victims they killed. The following have all had films made about their adventures.

1. **Ned Kelly** was hanged for killing policemen. His last words were, "Such is life!" He believed he was fighting for freedom against the evil law officers, and many people have sympathy with that. Certainly Constable Fitzpatrick, who persecuted the Kelly family at first, was sacked from the police force for being a "liar and a larrikin". Kelly was a typical outlaw legend; he used his knowledge of the countryside to hide from and dodge and ambush the law officers. He is more of a national hero than a national villain in Australia.

2. **Bonnie and Clyde** Bonnie Parker (1910–34) and Clyde Barrow (1909–34) were legendary American outlaws. During their bank raids they murdered twelve people, yet they are remembered for their daring and cheek. Clyde Barrow's favourite car was a Ford V8 – he stole them whenever he could and had the insolence to write to the maker, Henry Ford, *While I have still got breath in my lungs I will tell you what a dandy car you make. I have drove Fords exclusively when I could get away with one. For sustained speed and freedom from trouble the Ford has got every other car skinned.* And Bonnie did some writing too – shortly before her death she wrote this poem:

> *Some day they will go down together*
> *And they will bury them side by side.*
> *To a few it means grief*
> *To the law it's relief*
> *But it's death to Bonnie and Clyde.*

Almost right . . . following their deaths in a final gun battle, they were buried separately.

3. **Butch Cassidy** Robert Parker was the grandson of a bishop but he preferred shooting and rustling to religion. He changed his name to Cassidy after one of his outlaw friends, and was nicknamed Butch because he'd worked in a butcher shop. In 1896 more than a hundred outlaws were hiding in Brown's Hole. They elected Cassidy as their leader and called themselves The Wild Bunch. They robbed banks, trains and mining stations. Cassidy carried a gun but it's said he never shot anyone. He escaped with his friend Harry Longabaugh (also known as the Sundance Kid) to Argentina. But when they tried robbing a Bolivian mining station they were trapped by detectives. In the shoot-out Sundance was killed. Some believe that Cassidy escaped and lived to old age, but no one knows for sure.

4. **William H. Bonney** (1859–81) He was also known as Billy the Kid. Legend has it that Billy the Kid killed his first victim when he was just twelve years old. He grew to be handsome, well-dressed and popular with women. He was also a ruthless killer. The

authorities believed in the old saying "Set a thief to catch a thief," and hired an old friend of Billy's, Pat Garrett, to track him down. Garrett captured Billy, who was tried and sentenced to death, only to escape from Lincoln jail. Garrett traced him again: this time there was no trial and no jail. Garrett shot him. Billy the Kid had nineteen notches on his gun – one for every man he killed, though he probably killed more. A monument was put up on the spot where he died. Pat Garrett made money by writing a book . . . on the Life of Billy the Kid!

5.   **Robin Hood** Records show that a man lived in Wakefield, England, who could be the source of the Robin Hood legend. He was christened Robert Hood in about 1290. He fought for his lord against King Edward II but lost and had to flee into Barnsdale Forest. The Great North Road ran through this forest, so it was an ideal spot for a gang of robbers to live and hide. A story published in 1429 (*A Lytell Geste of Robyn Hood*) tells of Hood's gang meeting Edward II in Nottingham in 1323 and making their peace with him. It is true that the king was there at the time. And the household accounts of the next year show a record of wages paid to Robin Hood. Those are the facts. We will never know how many of the other stories about him are true. What makes Robin Hood so memorable and popular is the legend that he robbed the rich and gave to the poor.

Not all outlaws terrorised the land. Some of the most famous were outlaws of the sea.

PIRªTES
The
"Fame's Revenge"

Pirates lived rough and violent lives. The trouble is that if you live outside the rule of law, you can't expect your friends and enemies to fight by any rule. They'd as soon stab you in the back as fight you fairly . . .

The Atlantic Coast of America, June 1726

The little man grinned and showed a row of broken, yellow teeth. "I'm going to be the greatest pirate that ever sailed the seas," he said. "I am William Fly . . . and you, Mr Atkinson, have the honour of being my first prisoner."

A tall man sat at the cabin table, his wrists chained in bands of iron. He looked at the little pirate calmly. "It is indeed an honour," he said carefully. "Have you been a pirate for long?"

Fly stood up. The cabin ceiling was low yet the top of his greasy-haired head didn't reach it. "Two weeks! I was a slave trader before that! Sailed under Captain Green. We used to go down to Guinea and make a deal with a tribe of natives down there. The natives attacked their neighbours, captured them and sold them to us. We sold the slaves in Jamaica for a hundred times the price we paid!"

"A good trade," Atkinson said quietly.

Fly's face twisted in anger as he remembered. "Not so very good. More than half the slaves died before we could sell them." He spat on the filthy wooden floor of the cabin.

"So piracy pays better?"

"It will!" Fly promised. "You saw how easily we captured your ship!" he crowed.

"We were an unarmed trading vessel," Atkinson reminded him.

The pirate suddenly flew at the seaman and slapped his face viciously. "Are you saying I'm a coward? Are you saying we wouldn't attack if you were armed? Are you? Are you?" Flecks of white foam frothed at the edge of his cracked lips and purple spots of rage burned his weathered face.

Atkinson shook his head slowly. "I'm sure you're a very brave man, Mr Fly . . ."

"*Captain!*" the little pirate screeched. "*Captain* Fly! You bet I'm brave! I used to be a boxer, you know! Back in Bristol I beat men twice my size, *and* Captain Green that owned this ship, the *Fame's Revenge*! He was twice my size!"

The little man's nostrils were wide and he breathed heavily, but he was slowly calming down.

Atkinson looked at him warily. His life depended on keeping the little maniac calm. "And what happened to Captain Green?"

"He was vicious, was Captain Green. Had the men flogged at the drop of a hat. The men hated him! So I led a mutiny. I crept up on him in his cabin and held a cutlass to his throat. He wasn't such a big man then – begged for his life!"

"And did you spare him?"

"Spare him? Set him free to give evidence against me? Set him free to see me hang for mutiny? Do I look stupid, Mr Atkinson?"

"You look a very clever man, Mr . . . er, Captain Fly!" Atkinson lied.

Fly sat down at the table and said softly, "I played fair with Captain Green. I gave him a choice. I said he could jump over the side of the ship, or he could be thrown over the side!"

Fly's breath stank but Atkinson tried not to show his disgust. "And which did he choose?"

The pirate sneered, "He refused to jump. We threw him. But he had a choice, didn't he?"

"And are you going to give me a choice?" Atkinson asked.

"I am. You can join my crew – or you can die!"

Atkinson leaned forward. "Captain Fly, it would be an honour to fight for you!"

"Schooner off the starboard bow, Captain!" the lookout called.

Fly reached for his telescope. "Aye, and it isn't armed! Easy meat. Run up a flag to show we're in distress," he ordered.

A large man with a tangled beard lumbered along the deck towards the pirate captain. "But we're not in distress, Captain," he said.

Fly snatched a pistol from his belt and waved it under the man's nose. "It's a trick, Alex Mitchell! A trick! They'll see our flag of distress. They'll stop to help us, then we'll climb aboard and attack them!"

"Right, Captain." Mitchell nodded stupidly and set about giving orders for the flag to be hoisted up the mast.

The pirate ship wallowed in the choppy sea as Fly paced the bridge. The little man looked up to the lookout. "What's happening?"

"The schooner's putting on more sail, Captain," the man called down. "It's running away!"

Fly snatched his cutlass from his belt and stormed down to the deck. "Hoist the sails! We're going after her!"

He slapped the scurrying sailors with the flat of his cutlass. At the foremast Will Atkinson smiled and pulled patiently on a rope. He spoke quietly to the sailor beside him – one of his shipmates from the old ship. "That schooner is the *James*. If Fly thinks the captain of the *James* is stupid enough to fall for the distress flag trick then he's a bigger idiot than he looks. Those days as a boxer must have softened his brain!"

His shipmate smiled. "It's just a matter of time, Will – just a matter of time."

He tightened the rope and looked over the bow of the pirate ship. The schooner was coming closer. Fly was racing around giving orders. "Fire the cannon! Fire the cannon! But don't hit the schooner! Don't hit it! I want it all in one piece! It'll be the second ship in my fleet! I'm going to be the greatest pirate that ever sailed the seas."

Will Atkinson and his shipmate watched as the schooner lowered its sails and waited for the pirate to come alongside. Frightened faces of unarmed fishermen appeared at the side of the vessel.

The pirate ship rushed towards the *James*, then veered away just before it struck the fishing schooner. "Lower the sails, you fools!" Fly screamed.

Will Atkinson shook his head. "Captain Fly couldn't sail a kite," he said quietly. "He'll never be able to bring us alongside the *James* without wrecking us both!"

"All hands on deck!" the hulking Alex Mitchell called. "The captain wants to talk to you!"

Will moved forward and was careful to stand in a group with six sailors who'd been captured with him on Fly's first attack. "Now, men," the pirate captain shouted above the slapping of the waves over the deck. "The sea's too rough for us to pull alongside that schooner. I want six men to take the ship's boat and row across. Take command – they won't fight. If they do, they know I'll blow them out of the water with our cannon."

"I'll go, captain!" Alex Mitchell called.

"Good man! Anyone going with him gets the largest share of the valuables," the little man promised slyly.

A group of five other men rushed forward quickly. Will and his six friends stood silent as the pirates lowered a rowing boat into the sea. They looked at one another and spoke quietly. "Only three of Fly's men left on board."

"It's the best chance we'll have."

"But Fly's armed. He has half a dozen pistols on the bridge beside him – and that cutlass in his belt."

"Hush!" Will said. "I've thought of all that, and I have a plan . . ."

"Captain! A whole fleet of schooners ahead!" Will Atkinson cried from the bows of the ship.

Fly snatched his telescope and squinted at the horizon. "Where, Atkinson?"

"I can see them from here, Captain. Unarmed as far as I can tell! Moving slowly . . . they must be loaded with goods. What prizes!"

"Where? Where? I can't see any schooners!"

"No, Captain, you have to come here," one of Will's shipmates cried from the capstan that held the anchor.

Fly grasped his telescope and left the safety of his bridge and the armoury of loaded pistols. "What a prize!" he muttered as he hurried forward, his feet slapping on the damp decks. "What a pirate!"

Will Atkinson was waiting for him. He gripped Fly excitedly by the wrist. The right wrist. The wrist that could have snatched the cutlass. This was the signal his shipmates were waiting for. They stepped forward. One slapped a hand over Fly's open mouth and the other pinned his arms behind him.

Will Atkinson sprinted along the deck, leapt up onto the bridge and grabbed one of the pirate's pistols.

Beneath the deck Fly's pirates heard the running and climbed the stairs to see what was going on. As the first raised his head above the deck Will Atkinson brought the handle of the pistol smashing down on his skull. The man fell onto the deck with a small cry like an injured puppy. "Here!" the second pirate gasped. "Don't hit me! I give up."

Will turned the pistol round so that the barrel was pointing at the man. "And did you have mercy on Captain Green?" he asked.

The pirate's face twisted in fear. "I'm not jumping over-board! I can't swim!"

"No," Will Atkinson said grimly. "But you can *swing* – you can swing from the end of a rope!"

A month later, just two months after William Fly had turned pirate, he was hanged in Boston with two of his crew . . . though the pirate cook was pardoned.

Fly enjoyed his one moment of fame as a pirate. He stood on the gallows holding bouquets of flowers, bowing and laughing at spectators.

Pirates – FACT FILE

1.   There have been pirates for almost as long as there have been sailors. One of the earliest recorded acts of piracy was the kidnap of the Roman leader, Julius Caesar. Pirates held him imprisoned until his friends paid a ransom of fifty talents. Caesar left captivity swearing to avenge himself. He returned with an army, captured the pirates and had them crucified.

2.   Sea robbers haven't always been criminals. When a country was at war it would employ private ship-owners – "privateers" – to attack enemy ships. They could rob the enemy as much as they liked, so long as they gave a share to their government. But when the war was over the "privateers" would be called "pirates" and hanged if they were caught!

3.   Pirates would fly a black flag as a signal that the enemy should surrender and be treated mercifully. If the enemy ignored the black flag then a red flag was flown – a sign that they would be attacked and no mercy would be shown.

4.   No one can agree on why the pirate flag is known as the "Jolly Roger". It has been suggested that the name comes from:
• the French *Jolie Rouge* or "Pretty Red" flag
• the English "Jolly Rogues"
• the Asian-Indian *Ali Raja*, King of the Sea.
Not many Jolly Roger flags had a skull and crossbones on them. The designs varied depending on the pirate. They included:
• a skull and crossed swords
• a skull and hourglass – the hourglass being a sign that your time was running out
• a body with a dart in the heart and three drops of blood
• a skeleton of a devil with a spear and a bleeding heart.

5.   Here are some pirate facts and fantasies. It's true that pirates wore gold earrings because they believed they gave you better eyesight! It's also true that pirates sent a "black spot" – or an ace of spades playing card – as a death threat to traitors; today we still talk of someone being "on the spot", meaning in a threatening situation. But *no* pirate ever made a man "walk the plank" – except in books and films! They did tell

—captives they were "free to walk home" when they were miles from shore, but there is no record of a plank ever being used.

6.   Pirates in the Caribbean bought strips of dried, smoked meat to take with them on their voyages. The men on the island of Hispaniola who smoked the meat were called "boucaniers" – meat-smokers. The pirates, who bought a hundred strips of the meat for six pieces of eight, became known as "boucaniers" too. The word later became "buccaneers". Other names for pirates through the centuries have been:
• "corsair", from the Spanish word for pirate
• "freebooter", because they got their "booty" free
• "filibuster", from the French for freebooter
• "sea rover" and "sea robber" from the German and Dutch.

7.   The cruellest – and most famous – pirate was probably Edward Teach, known the world over as Blackbeard. Legend has it that he:
• plaited his beard so it looked as if he had snakes crawling over his face
• twisted burning rope into his hair so he terrified the enemy when he attacked
• was capable of splitting a man in two with one stroke of his cutlass
• had fourteen wives
• carried six pistols on each side at all times
• shot his Mate, Israel Hands, in the knee and crippled him for life, just for fun.

Blackbeard was finally betrayed by Israel Hands and cornered by a British naval vessel. Despite twenty-five bullet and cutlass wounds he fought on. When he finally died of his wounds his head was cut off and nailed to the front of the ship. His body was thrown overboard – the legend is that the headless body swam round the ship several times before it finally sank! Hands died, a beggar on the London streets, but his name lives on as a character in Robert Louis Stevenson's book *Treasure Island*.

8. The owners of some unarmed whaling ships painted the sides of their ships to look as if they had cannon on board. This was to scare off pirates.

9. There were several famous women pirates. Anne Bonny and Mary Read fought as fiercely and skilfully as their male comrades. Mary once took her lover's place in a duel – and won. Mary Read died in prison but Anne Bonny, the daughter of a wealthy lawyer, was probably never captured.

The cruellest woman pirate was possibly Maria Cobbham, who wore the uniform of a dead naval officer she had killed. She was more interested in killing than in loot – she once used three captured sailors for pistol-shooting target practice!

The Chinese woman Ching Shih commanded a vast pirate navy in the early years of the nineteenth century. At one time she had nearly 2000 boats and 80,000 sailors fighting for her.

10.   Not all pirates died at the end of a hangman's rope. Some lived to be old, wealthy and respectable. Henry Morgan once led the biggest force of buccaneers ever seen in the West Indies. In later years, he was knighted by Charles II, sent back to the West Indies as Governor of Jamaica, and given the job of capturing and punishing pirates!

Lancelot Blackburne became Archbishop of York in 1700. However, he was often embarrassed by visits from old shipmates. He'd been a pirate in the West Indies in the 1680s.

HIGHWAYMEN
Rogues
Of The Road

Some criminals become popular, even when they are robbing and killing people. They become legends and heroes and the stories about them get wildly exaggerated. Criminals like Robin Hood, Billy the Kid, Bonnie and Clyde and, of course, the highwaymen . . .

The London-to-Cambridge Road, 1736

The moon drifted out from behind the clouds and lit the London Road. The muddy trail ran like a silver ribbon through the blackness of the forest.

At the edge of the forest a man sat on his horse and shivered. The horse was well trained and stood perfectly still and silent while the man shrugged himself deeper into his dark woollen cloak and tightened the handkerchief round his neck to keep out the chill draught.

He sighed and murmured to his patient horse, "It looks like we're out of luck tonight."

He tugged the rein and walked out onto the road. The horse stopped suddenly and snorted. "What is it, girl?" the rider asked. The horse had sensed something. The rider peered down the road and saw a shadow moving down the moonlit track. "Ah! A victim!"

It was too late to slip back into the forest so the rider waited at the side of the road and let the stranger trot nearer. Then he pulled the handkerchief up until it covered the lower half of his face. When the stranger was just a few paces away the masked man dug his spurs into his horse's flank and the animal jumped forward into the middle of the road. The robber pulled two pistols from his belt. Their black muzzles were darker than death. "Stand and deliver!" he cried.

The stranger looked startled. He gripped his reins tightly and calmed his frightened horse. The stranger was finely dressed and rich rings glinted on his fingers. He peered at the masked man. "It's the famous Dick Turpin, I presume," he said calmly.

It was the highwayman's turn to be startled. "You know me?"

"Everyone's heard of the famous Dick Turpin," the rich man smiled. "It's an honour to be robbed by you, sir!"

"Hand over your money," Turpin demanded roughly.

The stranger smiled. "This is not your usual road, Mr Turpin. I didn't expect to see you here tonight."

"Someone betrayed me to the law officers. I'm on my way from Essex."

"And where are you headed, Mr Turpin?"

"I'm going to . . ." the highwayman stopped suddenly. "That, sir, is none of your business. There is a reward of 100 guineas on my head. If I told you where I'm hiding then I'd have to kill you to keep you quiet," he said viciously. "Now, hand over your rings!"

The rich man began to slide a gold ring from his finger. "My wedding ring," he sighed. He looked up at Turpin and smiled. "My wife gave it to me. She will be so disappointed to know that I lost it."

"That's nothing to me," the highwayman said coldly.

"Are you married, Mr Turpin?"

"Yes."

"Then spare a thought for my wife, good sir."

"I want that ring!"

"And you shall have it!" the rich man promised. "But do one thing for me in return. Put a bullet through my hat. When I show my wife the bullet hole she'll be so glad that I'm alive she'll forget about the ring."

Turpin shrugged and raised the pistol in his left hand. The rich man held his hat well away from his body. Turpin fired and the bullet tore a ragged hole in the felt, three-cornered hat.

The stranger smiled. "Thank you, sir. If you could place

another shot through my cloak I could say I struggled with you in a great fight! I would be a hero with my whole town!"

Turpin gave a sudden laugh and fired carefully at the man's cloak. "The rings?" he asked.

"One last favour . . . a bullet through this handkerchief," he said, sliding a hand inside his coat.

"No!" the highwayman growled. "My pistols are empty."

The stranger nodded and pulled his hand from under the coat. And in his hand he held a pistol. "Ah, Mr Turpin, but *this* pistol is *not* empty!"

Turpin scowled and threw his useless weapon onto the path. The stranger laughed and put his pistol away. "Fooled you, eh?"

"What's so funny? I suppose you'll shoot me."

"What? Dog eat dog? No, young Dick. You simply made the mistake of trying to rob a robber!"

"You're a robber?"

The rich man nodded and moved his horse closer. "Allow me to introduce myself. I'm the highwayman Tom King."

Turpin leaned forward in his saddle and shook the man's hand. "Why, Mr King . . . of course I've heard of you! I apologise for this mistake!"

King laughed. "I think perhaps you owe me a little hospitality. Is your hideout near here?"

"Follow me!" Turpin cried. Turning his horse sharply he galloped through the dark and secret forest paths while Tom King raced to keep up with him. At last they came to a clearing where a fire lit the mouth of a large cave. Turpin leapt down from his horse and left it to graze on the turf. He threw an arm around his wife and said, "We have a guest . . . meet Tom King!" And the highwayman told the tale of his meeting.

As they ate a stew of rabbit and vegetables King looked around the cave. "A wonderful hiding place."

"Plenty of food to poach in the forest," Mrs Turpin said.

"And plenty of rich travellers on the Cambridge Road," her husband agreed.

"Enough rich pickings for two highwaymen?" King asked carefully.

Turpin nodded eagerly. "Two men could earn ten times as much! Would you consider working with me?"

King sucked at a piece of rabbit meat between his teeth. "We could make a fortune . . . partner!" he said finally.

And so the two became the most frightening pair of villains in the south of England. Even indoors people weren't safe from King and Turpin. Then, a year later, in May 1737, Turpin rode to meet his friend in a tavern to plan another robbery.

He galloped through the forest then slowed to a trot as he reached the edge of the town. The horse stopped suddenly as if it sensed danger. Turpin slid down from the saddle and patted it on the neck. "Hush! It's only a crowd of people. Probably a drunken fight in the tavern!" The highwayman tied the horse to a tree and walked towards the edge of the crowd. "What's happening?" he asked a woman huddled in a dirty shawl.

"Ooooh! They say the landlord's captured that highwayman Tom King! There's a reward! King's been stealing horses!"

"Really!" Turpin gasped. "How evil! I've never seen this King! Reckon I could get a look at him?"

The woman leaned towards Turpin. "Sam's holding him at pistol point in the kitchen, they reckon."

"And is there a window in this kitchen?"

"Oh, yes! Here, I'll show you!" she offered.

He followed her to the side alley where people crowded and gossiped. "Here! get out of the way!" the woman squawked importantly. "There's a gentleman here come to have a look at our prisoner!" The poor people of the town shuffled aside as Turpin pushed his way through, scowling.

35

At last he reached the shuttered window and looked in. The red-faced landlord sat with his back to the door and smirked at Tom King. "Law officers be here soon, King. They'll hang you and I'll collect the reward."

"There are worse things than hanging," King shrugged. His back was to the window and he couldn't see Turpin standing behind him.

The landlord's ugly face clouded with doubt. "What's worse than hanging?" he demanded.

"Dying by slow poisoning," King said. "That's how your customers will die after drinking the filth you call ale!"

The landlord's face turned purple with rage. He raised the old pistol and pointed it at King's heart.

Turpin grabbed for the pistol at his belt. He raised it and pushed it through the window. At the same moment King leapt to his feet. He jumped between Turpin and the landlord. But Turpin's finger had already squeezed the trigger.

The powder in the pistol exploded. The bullet hit Turpin's friend in the back.

Tom King staggered and turned. His face was pale with shock. His eyes became glassy. "Dick!" he managed to groan before he slid to the sawdust floor of the tavern kitchen.

The townspeople scattered when they heard the shot. No one tried to stop Turpin as he raced for his horse.

He'd begun the friendship by trying to rob Tom King – he ended it by shooting him.

Highwaymen – FACT FILE

1.   Turpin was so upset by the death of his partner that he gave up highway robbery and retired to a Yorkshire village, where he called himself John Palmer. However, within a year he was in trouble for stealing sheep and horses. He might have escaped with a fine or a short jail sentence if he hadn't written to his brother for help. He forgot to pay the postage and his brother didn't recognise the writing and refused to pay for the letter. But the village schoolmaster *did* recognise the writing – a boy in his class had written like that many years ago . . . and his name was Dick Turpin! The teacher hurried to York, where he claimed the reward for bringing Turpin to justice. The highwayman was hanged in 1739.

2.   A book called *Rookwood* describes Dick Turpin's famous ride from London to York on his brave mare, Black Bess. Turpin escaped the law with that ride but poor Black Bess died. Many people still believe that this is a true story. The fact is that Turpin never owned a horse called Black Bess and never made such a ride. It is possible that another highwayman, John Nevison, made a similar ride.

3.   Many highway robbers worked on foot. They were known as footpads. Horses allowed you to cover a wider area and made for a fast getaway, but were expensive to feed and stable and difficult to disguise. The legend grew up that footpads were rough and cruel

while highwaymen were polite gentlemen, because only gentlemen could afford horses. This was not true!

4. Some poems and books depict highwaymen as generous Robin Hoods of the road. A folk song, "Brennan on the Moor", describes a highwayman as follows:

A pair of loaded pistols did he carry night and day,
He never robbed a poor man on all the King's highway.
But what he'd taken from the rich, like Turpin and Black Bess,
He always did divide between the widows in distress.

(Notice how poor Black Bess has become a partner in Turpin's crime!)

Another legend that surrounds highwaymen is that they were handsome and loved by ladies. But portraits that survive show them as ugly with bad teeth and faces scarred by disease.

5. Claude Duval had a reputation for being a gentleman robber. The story goes that he once stopped a coach on Hounslow Heath, knowing the couple inside were carrying £400. The lady tried to cover her fear by playing a flageolet – a kind of flute. Duval took out a flute and accompanied her. He then asked her to dance with him and her husband agreed. After the dance, Duval reminded the husband that he hadn't been paid for the music. The highwayman was given a hundred pounds. "That's so generous," he said, "that I'll excuse

you the other three hundred". Nice story – probably totally untrue! Another version of this story says that Duval snatched a baby's feeding bottle because it was made of silver. That sort of greedy act is more believable.

6.   Hounslow Heath was a popular place for highway robbery. It was wild and covered with thick furze bushes and thorns. It was difficult to get to London without passing across its 6650 acres. The Heath was also a good place for duels and prize fights. Nowadays most of Hounslow Heath is covered by London's Heathrow airport.

7.   There were highwaywomen too. The most famous was Mary Frith, who died in 1659. She became a maidservant when she left home but hated it, so she dressed as a man and became a pickpocket and, later, a highwaywoman. She worked with a specially trained dog. One of her most important victims was the famous soldier General Fairfax. She wounded him and killed two of his horses before she escaped, only to be captured later. Though she was imprisoned she was so rich from her crimes that she managed to buy her freedom with the huge sum (in those days) of £2000. She was nicknamed Moll Cutpurse and a character named after her appeared in a play, *The Roaring Girl* in 1611.

8.   Businessmen tried to cheat the highwaymen by cutting bank notes in half before sending them in the

mail coach. If they were stolen they were worthless. They then sent the second half of the notes the next day. But highwaymen Hawkins and Simpson got wise to this and robbed mail coaches on consecutive days so as to collect both halves!

9.   Highway robbery was made possible by the invention of the flintlock pistol, which was light enough to be carried in one hand while the other controlled the horse. When its single shot was used up it would take half a minute to reload or it could be used as a short club.

10.   Highwayman Isaac Atkinson went to church and heard the parson preach "The day of the Lord cometh as a thief in the night." As the priest went home Atkinson robbed him. "I'm not going against the Bible," Atkinson explained. "I come as a thief in the day!"

Robbery on the road is one of the oldest crimes. Remember the story of The Good Samaritan, who rescued a victim in the Bible story? It is also one of the newest crimes – nowadays it takes place on streets and is called "mugging". But the age of the mounted highwaymen really lasted from the Elizabethan times until Victorian times. Their peak was when coach journeys from London increased from six a day in 1662 to 119 a day just twenty years later. The invention of the railway put an end to the age of the highwayman. Trains are harder to catch and harder to stop . . .

THIEVES
The Great
Train Robbery

Robberies happen every second of every day. There are so many that no one could ever count the cost. Yet some robberies are remembered because they are bigger and more daring than most. One in England became famous as "The Great Train Robbery" . . .

Buckinghamshire, England, 1963

"Go to jail!" Cordrey chuckled.

Biggs scowled and moved his piece along the Monopoly board until he arrived in jail.

"That's the story of my life," he grumbled. "In and out of jail . . ." he looked at the small pile of paper beside him, ". . . and never any money."

Cordrey smiled and picked up a fistful of his winnings. "Not after tonight, Biggs! After tonight you'll have more money than this." He pointed to the board. "You can have a flat in Mayfair and a whole street of houses in Park Lane."

"I've got to get out of jail first," his partner said.

"No jail, Biggs. This is the best planned operation you've ever taken part in. Nothing can go wrong!"

Biggs looked at the paper in his hand. "You realise our fingerprints are all over this stuff – all over this farmhouse, in fact. The police will find it in the end. It's all one big clue!"

Cordrey grasped the other man's wrist and shook it. "How many times . . .? It's all sorted out. We're paying some lads to come and clean the place from top to bottom. They're professionals! Anyway, the police might not even find this hideout. It's twenty-five miles from where we're doing the robbery. This time tomorrow we'll be counting real money!"

Biggs looked at his watch. "Eight hours to go."

"That's right. The train'll just be leaving Glasgow now."

Jack Mills pushed the throttle on locomotive D326, released the brake and felt the cab judder as the engine took the strain of pulling the loaded coaches. It moved slowly out of Glasgow station and the rhythm of the clattering track became steady.

Jack wiped his brow and looked at his fireman, David Whitby. "This engine's not right, you know."

"Still wanting to go back to the old steam locomotives, Grandad?" David joked.

"No, I don't mean that," the driver said seriously. "I don't mind these diesels. Much easier than steam. No, I mean this particular engine doesn't *feel* right."

"Same as any other to me," the fireman said.

"It's unlucky, for a start," the driver argued.

"You what?"

"Mark my words. This engine's jinxed. You remember that crash at Crewe earlier this year?"

"Yeah. Mid-Day Scot crashed into the Liverpool-Birmingham train," David said as he checked the instruments in front of him. "About a dozen killed."

"Eighteen, to be exact," Jack said. "And thirty or more injured."

"So?"

"So, this was the locomotive that was pulling the Mid-Day Scot! Loco D326."

"That was different! It was a foggy night – and icy. The driver probably had trouble seeing the signals. You worry too much, Jack. There's nothing can go wrong tonight!" David assured him.

"You just keep your eyes on those signals!"

"You see, Biggs, nothing can go wrong!" Cordrey spoke softly as they lay by the trackside. They were dressed in army commando gear with their faces blackened. "Even if the police had stopped us we'd have said we were on an army exercise.

And we were driving Landrovers and an army truck. See! Reynolds thinks of everything."

"It's all right for you," Biggs complained. "You've got a real job to do. You're an expert on these trackside signals. But Reynolds only brought me in because I knew someone who could drive the train."

"You worry too much, mate. Now, what time do you make it?"

"Two minutes to three."

"That's right. Now, I'll just switch these wires, see . . ." and the green trackside lamp turned to amber. "Now let's get to the next one and turn it red."

Cordrey rose and began to move down the track. After a few paces he turned and looked at Biggs, who was struggling to pull another man after him. "What's wrong?" Cordrey hissed.

"He won't budge!" Biggs panted.

Cordrey trotted back and helped Biggs pull the struggling man. "We need this miserable little bleeder to drive the train! What's wrong with him?"

"I think he's scared," Biggs answered as they dragged the rigid man over the stony edge of the track. When they reached the next trackside signal Biggs sank to the ground while Cordrey worked on the wiring.

"You'd better have him sorted out before that train arrives!"

"I don't think he's going to make it," Biggs groaned. "And you said nothing could go wrong!"

"Amber light, Jack!" David called.

The driver had been quietly wrapped in his own thoughts and looking forward to a cup of tea when he reached London. He reached for the brake and the wheels screeched as the engine slowed.

"Slow down, Jack!" the fireman said urgently. "I think that's a red signal further ahead. Could be a stationary train on the track."

The driver snorted. "Like the Liverpool-to-Birmingham train this thing hit before? I thought you didn't believe in the jinx!"

"Yes, it's red. Stop, Jack!"

The train stopped. The cab trembled with the beat of the powerful engine. Otherwise there was silence.

David fixed his eye on that red light, waiting for it to change to green. A minute passed. "They won't be happy in London if we're late. Not when we're carrying High Value Packages," Jack said.

"What's in them?"

The driver shook his head. "Money, they reckon. Of course they don't tell us!"

"Want me to phone the signal box?"

"Yeah. Go on!"

The fireman opened the door of the cab and climbed down the iron steps to the ground. Jack heard his partner call, "What's up, mate?" then there was a scuffling on the grass outside.

Jack went to the door to investigate. A blackened face appeared. The driver backed away. Someone was climbing in the other door. He rushed at the second man but the first man was in the cab now and hitting him with an iron bar. The second blow to the skull knocked him senseless.

"What did you do that for, Edwards?" Cordrey yelled.

"He's in the way!"

"We need him!"

"What for?"

"To drive the train – they've uncoupled the coach with the money. Now we need to drive it to the bridge where the lorry's waiting."

"But that's why Ronnie Biggs brought a driver."

"He's hopeless. Scared. We can't even get him into the cab. No, this driver will have to do it."

The men hauled Jack Mills to his feet and shook him. "Come on, son. You're going to drive us just a quarter mile!"

Jack struggled to speak. "Red light . . . crash . . . unlucky loco!"

"No, son. This is our *lucky* loco!" Cordrey grinned. "It's going to make us rich!"

"Two million, six hundred and thirty-one pounds!" Biggs breathed.

"Didn't I tell you nothing could go wrong?" Cordrey crowed as they looked at the piles of bank notes on the table. "A hundred and fifty thousand each! . . . Hey, Biggs, fancy a game of Monopoly with real money?"

The robber picked up a counter in a daze, placed it on the board and shook the dice. "Oh dear, oh dear," Cordrey chuckled. "Go to jail, Biggs! Go to jail!"

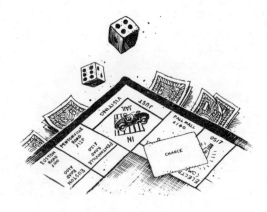

The Great Train Robbery – FACT FILE

1.   The farmhouse hideout was never cleaned by the train robbers' accomplices. Police found fingerprints everywhere, but particularly on the Monopoly game the robbers had played.

2.   Within a year most of the robbers were in jail.

3.   The attack on Jack Mills counted against the robbers. The judge gave them particularly heavy sentences because they had used violence in the robbery.

4.   Cordrey pleaded guilty and received the lightest sentence – fourteen years. He was released after seven.

5.   Biggs received one of the heaviest sentences – thirty years.

6.   Biggs escaped from prison and went to live in Brazil. He was once kidnapped and taken to British territory so that he could be returned to a British prison. The judge set him free to return to Brazil because the kidnapping was illegal.

7.   The public remember Biggs as a sort of hero who outwitted the police.

8.   The public forget poor Jack Mills. He never recovered from the beating he received and never worked again. He refused to blame the attack for his

failing health, but he died seven years after the robbery from leukaemia.

9.   In total the train robbers received 307 years in prison. Curiously, this made the public feel sorry for them. Edwards, who coshed Jack Mills, even had a film, *Buster*, made of his story.

10.   The jinxed loco D326 caused more misery before it was scrapped. In 1964 a railwayman on its roof was electrocuted by overhead wires. In 1965 its brakes failed and it crashed into a freight train, injuring the guard. As soon as its number was changed to 40126 it began to behave.

Punishments – FACT FILE

Punishments are a way of taking revenge on a criminal. They can also be a way of stopping the criminal from breaking the law again – a burglar can't steal while in prison and a murderer can't kill again after execution! Punishments are also a way of telling people, "This is what will happen to you if you try to do the same." Throughout history some punishments have been more unusual than others . . .

1. King Gustav III of Sweden was convinced that coffee was a poison. To prove his point he sentenced a murderer to death by drinking coffee every day. And to show he was right the king ordered another murderer to drink tea every day. Two doctors were given the task of checking the experiment. The doctors died first! The king was murdered in 1792, the tea-drinker died many years later at the age of 83 and the coffee-drinker survived them all!

2. Saint Catherine was sentenced to death for being a Christian. Her method of execution was to be tied to a spiked wheel and rolled down a hill. We remember this today with the spinning firework known as a Catherine Wheel.

3. Many animals have been brought to trial and punished for their crimes. The Bible says, "If an ox gore a man or a woman so that they die then the ox shall surely be stoned." (Exodus). In the year 864 a hive of bees which stung a man to death was condemned to be suffocated. In 1906 a Swiss dog was charged, along with

two men, of murder. The men got life imprisonment but the dog was condemned to death. In 1974 in Italy a dog that bit a man was sentenced to a month in prison on a diet of bread and water – it served the sentence and was released. Even today vicious dogs can be put down, but their owners usually end up with a fine for failing to control them.

4. One of the first law books ever to be written was that of Hammurabi, King of Babylon. Among the rules there are some which tell doctors what they can treat, and what will happen to them if the treatment goes wrong. For example, if a doctor accidentally killed a patient while opening an abscess then he was sentenced to have his hands cut off.

5. In 1890 the Emperor of Abyssinia, Menelek II, decided to modernise the criminal justice system. He ordered three electric chairs from the United States for executions. Then he discovered that you needed electricity to make them work. There was no electricity in Abyssinia at that time, so he got rid of two chairs and kept the third as his throne.

6. Many US states abolished the death penalty (or were unwilling to use it) in the twentieth century. Murderer Michael Godwin was sentenced to death in the electric chair in South Carolina in 1988. He appealed and the punishment was changed to life imprisonment. However, one day he accidentally bit through a wire as he tried to mend the headphones on

his television set. He was sitting on the cell's metal toilet seat and was electrocuted and died.

7.   A modern method of checking on a criminal is to fit him or her with an electronic radio transmitter. Law officers can tune in at any time and check where the criminal is. This is not a new idea, however. In Europe in the Middle Ages a criminal could be made to wear a collar with a bell attached, suspended over the head. This marked the criminal out, but the constant jangling probably drove him crazy!

8.   Not everyone trusts the law to punish criminals. Some people prefer to take the law into their own hands. During the 1930s the banks were so fed up with bank-robbing gangs that they put up vicious Wanted posters. One read:

$5000 REWARD
FOR DEAD BANK ROBBERS!!
THE ASSOCIATION WILL NOT GIVE ONE CENT FOR LIVE BANK ROBBERS

9.   Not all judges are saints. Judge Roy Bean had been a smuggler before he became a bar-keeper and

gambler in Vinegaroon, Texas. He then got the job of town judge and would often stop trials to serve liquor to the lawyers and even the criminals. He'd also take a break to play cards when he felt like it. He once had to act as coroner and give a verdict on the cause of death when a worker fell 100 metres from a building. He didn't think the coroner's $5 fee was enough, so he searched the body and found $40 and a gun. He pocketed the cash, declaring, "I find this corpse guilty of carrying a concealed weapon, and I fine it $40!"

10. Some criminals spend a long, long time in jail. Paul Geidel went to jail in New York in 1912 – he came out 68 years, 8 months and two days later in 1980. He died in 1987, having spent just 25 of his 93 years as a free man. Bill Wallace spent the last 63 years of his life in an Australian prison, where he died in 1989 just before his 108th birthday.

TRICKSTERS
The $100,000
Bucket Of Water

You can't sell something if you don't own it, or if it doesn't even exist! But that doesn't stop some people trying. It's called fraud.

Farmingdale, New York, USA, April 1916

"Careful! This bottle contains the deadliest poison known to mankind!" the old man whispered.

The young newspaper reporter licked his lips and his hand began to tremble. He unscrewed the top of the bottle. A sharp smell, like almonds, stung his nose and made his eyes water. "Bring that bucket closer, Morton!" he hissed to another reporter.

Morton lifted his hat and wiped the sweat from his brow with the back of his sleeve. He slid the bucket across the garage floor. "There you are, Wilson."

Wilson carefully tipped the green liquid into the bucket of water and watched it turn cloudy. He put the top back on the bottle and placed it on the table as carefully as if it were a bomb.

The old man nodded. "You see, Mr Morton? A bucket of water. You filled it yourself from the tap, yes?"

"Yes, Professor Enricht. Pure water," Morton nodded slowly. His sharp brown eyes narrowed. This had to be a trick.

The old professor raised his thick, grey eyebrows, "And you have examined the car, Mr Wilson?"

The reporter said, "I'm no mechanic, prof, but there's no petrol in that petrol tank."

"And there is no hidden petrol tank in the car?"

Wilson raised one shoulder. "Not that I can find."

The old man looked pleased. "So. We will pour the water into the petrol tank. We will start the car, and you will drive it, yes?" His English was good but he had a strong German accent.

"No, professor. Cars don't run on water," Morton sneered.

"They run on water that has my secret liquid in it," Louis

Enricht smiled. "Mr Morton! Pour the water into the petrol tank."

Morton snatched at the bucket and some of the deadly liquid slopped over the side. He felt the old man was making a fool of him, but he couldn't work out how or why. The man who could make cars run on water would be worth millions and millions of dollars. Especially now. With the Great War raging in Europe there was a shortage of petrol.

"Careful! It's poison!" young Wilson squeaked, jumping away from the splashes.

"Hah!" Morton snorted. "This is moonshine. We're fools for ever coming here."

It was true that all the New York papers had been invited to this exciting event. Only Morton and Wilson had bothered to come. Now young Wilson was scared and Morton was cursing himself for being such a fool. He took the metal funnel and carelessly poured the liquid into the tank.

"Now, Mr Wilson, perhaps you would take the wheel of the car . . . and you, Mr Morton, turn the starting handle."

The older reporter was fat and sweating and didn't want the work. "Can't you do it, professor?" he snapped.

The old man shook his head. "I do not want you to think there are any tricks at all. I do not want to touch the car!"

Morton took off his jacket and laid it carefully on the seat of the car. He rolled up his sleeves, spat on his hands and gripped the handle that stuck out from the front of the car. He swung it viciously. The car engine turned and spluttered and died. The reporter looked at the professor. The old man smiled back. "It will take a little while for the water to reach the engine."

Morton swung at the handle again. Nothing. Angry now, he whipped it round. Again. Nothing. Again. And again. Angry with himself, he gave it one last swing and staggered back as the engine coughed twice then clattered into life.

"Jump in!" young Wilson cried and his colleague scrambled into the open-topped two-seater.

The two men sailed out into the April sunshine with a cloud of almond-scented smoke trailing behind them. An hour later they pulled back into the garage.

"It's a miracle!" Wilson murmured.

"It's a trick," Morton growled.

"But how does he do it?" the younger reporter asked.

Morton shook his head angrily. "I don't know. But I know a man who would – Henry Ford himself!"

So the next visitor was Ford, the greatest car manufacturer in the world. "That smell. Almonds. It's cyanide, isn't it?"

Professor Enricht said softly, "You are a very intelligent man, Mr Ford. But you must understand that the secret is mine – until you buy it. The cyanide is only there to hide the smell of the real secret ingredient."

Ford sighed. "There is no trick, professor. How much do you want?"

"One million dollars. A hundred thousand now, the rest when you produce the liquid. Just think, Mr Ford. You will be hero to everyone in the United States – everyone in the world! Car fuel for a penny a gallon!"

The millionaire thought carefully. "I will give you ten thousand now and another ninety thousand when I've tried the formula myself."

The old man looked disappointed, but agreed. There was a strange smile on his face as he folded Ford's cheque and slipped it into his pocket. Half an hour later he picked up the telephone. "Mr Maxim? Enricht here. Mr Ford has just left. That's right . . . the great Mr Ford himself says my secret formula works. And if Henry Ford says its good, then it must be so! . . . Ah, no, he'll only give me half a million," the professor lied. "Yes, Mr

Maxim. I will sell it to you for one million dollars! When I have your hundred-thousand dollars deposit, I will send you the formula."

Henry Ford was furious when he discovered that the inventor had sold the secret to a higher bidder. But Enricht sent back the ten thousand dollar cheque and Ford could do nothing.

The old German now had a hundred thousand dollar fortune just for making a car run on a bucket of water.

But Maxim was too busy making guns for the war to go into business producing the magic liquid. He sold the idea to a banker called Yoakum. Yoakum paid Enricht *another* hundred thousand dollars and in return Enricht gave him an envelope with the secret inside.

Enricht said that the envelope must not be opened without his permission. Even the President of the USA was thrilled to think that his people would soon have the wonderful cheap fuel.

Then Enricht started to make excuses. "When can we have the fuel?" Yoakum demanded.

"Tomorrow, maybe. Next week, maybe," Enricht shrugged and smiled.

But "tomorrow" never came. Detectives reported that Enricht was a friend of the German ambassador – and the USA was at war with Germany. Was he a spy? Was this all a great trick to harm the USA?

Yoakum opened the envelope. It was full of worthless paper!

Enricht had made two hundred thousand dollars with a simple trick. Yoakum died before he could get his money back, or have Enricht thrown into jail.

Two years later Enricht died in jail. He had been imprisoned for another swindle that didn't work so well.

And, to this day, no one is quite sure how a seventy-year-old fraudster could trick the world's greatest motor manufacturer and the President of the United States of America.

'Fraud – FACT FILE

Because Yoakum had confidence *in Enricht, he gave him $100,000. This sort of swindle is known as a* confidence trick *and Enrich was an expert confidence trickster, or "con" man for short.*

But how did he make a car run on water? What was the magic liquid?

Enricht had come across a little known fact. A mixture of acetone and liquid acetylene will make a car run when it is mixed with water. It smells like nail varnish remover – a distinctive scent that anyone would recognise. You'd have to disguise that smell with another chemical such as cyanide!

So Enricht's magic mixture really did work, but that wasn't the trick. The trick was in promising to make petrol for a penny a gallon. Enricht's magic mixture cost much, much more to make than petrol – and it also ruins a car's engine after a while!

Enricht was a clever con man, but not the greatest or the most daring. Here are some of the most remarkable cases:

1. In 1925 Count Victor Lustig, a Czechoslovakian, gathered a group of businessmen together and told them that the Eiffel Tower in Paris was proving too expensive to run. He said that he had been given the job of selling it for scrap. The highest bidder could take it down. André Poisson bid several million francs and Lustig took his money. Poisson realised he had been stupid but didn't want the rest of France to know about it, so he didn't report the swindle to the police. Lustig got away with it, and a few years later sold the Eiffel Tower *again*! He then moved to the United States,

where he became a forger. In 1945 he was sentenced to twenty years in prison for making $134,000,000 by fraudulent means.

2. In 1925 Arthur Ferguson "sold" Buckingham Palace for £2000; Big Ben for £1000 and Nelson's Column for £6000. Later that year he moved to the United States where he rented out the President's White House for $100,000, but he was caught when he tried to "sell" the Statue of Liberty.

3. Four American con men robbed the Bank of England of over £100,000 in 1873. They were caught and sentenced to life imprisonment. One of the men then pulled the best con trick of all. George Bidwell had served only six years when he managed to convince the prison doctor that he was dying. He was released . . . and then made a wonderful recovery! His partners each served eighteen years.

4. In 1911 a con man, Valiferno, and an art forger, Chaudron, stole the famous Mona Lisa painting from the Louvre Gallery in France. They then made six copies of the painting and sold them to art collectors secretly. The collectors all thought they were getting the real painting for just $300,000, but they were breaking the law by buying a stolen painting, so they couldn't go to the police when they discovered they had paid a fortune for a fake. Chaudron and Valiferno pocketed the money and returned the painting two years later. It is still there, under much more careful guard!

5. In 1927 experts at the Cleveland Art Gallery in America discovered they had bought a fake sculpture. It wasn't the 700-year-old carving they believed at first – it was made by an Italian art forger called Dossena. They took the fake out of their exhibition and replaced it with a beautiful marble statue at a cost of $120,000 . . . then discovered that this was yet another Dossena fake!

6. In 1898 Louis de Rougement told a story which made him world famous. He described how he had spent the last thirty years among the Aborigines of Australia and lived to tell the tale. After being shipwrecked, he said, he'd taken part in cannibal feasts, built a house of shells, sent messages in the beaks of pelicans and ridden on the backs of monster turtles. De Rougement had his listeners fascinated with the tale of how he recovered from a deadly fever by sleeping with the body of a dead buffalo. He was invited to all the most important Scientific Societies in the world! His fame was so great that his waxwork figure was displayed at Madame Tussaud's in London. At last it was proved he was a fake. But Louis went on giving lectures in South Africa, describing himself as "The World's Greatest Liar".

7. In March 1854 an English lord, Sir Roger Tichborne, left England on board the ship *Bella*. The ship was never seen again. Roger's mother refused to believe her son was dead. She advertised for him to get in touch with her – and at last a letter arrived from Australia from a man claiming to be Roger. Lady

Henrietta Tichborne desperately wanted to believe this was her son. When the man arrived in England he was found to weigh a massive 24 stone (over 150 kilos) – Roger had weighed less than nine stone (under 60 kilos). Roger had straight dark hair and a tattoo on his left arm and spoke fluent French. The Australian had wavy fair hair, no tattoo, and did not speak a word of French. But Lady Henrietta explained away all these errors and granted her long-lost "son" a thousand pounds a year allowance! But when she died and the Australian tried to claim the family estates, he was taken to court and lost his case. He went to prison for ten years. The "son" turned out to be Arthur Orton, horse-thief and bankrupt. Still, he had brought happiness to old Henrietta . . . and someone else believed his ridiculous claim, because he is buried under a tombstone that reads "Sir Roger Tichborne, died 1 April 1898." A suitable date for a trickster to die, perhaps?

8.   Some people are easier to con than others and will believe anything! A woman was picking blackberries outside of the London prison, Wormwood Scrubs, when a rope ladder appeared followed by three escaping criminals. "We're just popping out for a cup of tea," they explained. "We'll be back later." She believed them and didn't bother to report the escape!

9.   Forgers don't only make bank-notes and works of art. They can forge poems, plays and books too. Teenager William Ireland claimed that he had found long-lost documents from William Shakespeare's pen,

then the long-lost script of one of his plays. The play was even performed at the famous Drury Lane Theatre in 1796 by the leading Shakespearian actor of that time, John Kemble. But Kemble saw through the trick and performed it as a joke. The play was laughed off the stage. Young Ireland confessed, but his old father could never believe that the treasured documents were fakes.

10.   The greatest con attempt ever was so amazing that it never had a chance of succeeding. In 1992 a 24-year-old Scotsman walked into a betting shop to claim his winnings. He said he'd correctly forecast the results of all the English and Scottish Football League games played on Boxing Day. To get the result of one game right would win you some money. To forecast eight correct results could win you more than a million pounds. He said he'd forecast all sixty-one results! The betting shop owed him four thousand, thousand, million pounds for his 50-pence bet! It was a trick, of course – the young man had taken advantage of a betting shop error to fill in the results *after* they'd happened. If he'd gone for a few thousand pounds he might have got away with it, but not that vast amount. When he was arrested he said it was "a bit of a joke, really". The judge said it was fraud. His girlfriend said, "He was going to buy us a bit of land – *Scot*land!"

KIDNaPPeRS
The
'Babysitter'

Kidnapping can be one of the cruellest crimes. If you are rich then you live with the fear that a stranger may snatch someone you love and threaten to kill them if you don't part with some of your riches . . .

Long Island, USA, 4 July 1956

Police Lieutenant Sam Barber looked at the note in his hand and read it for the tenth time or more. It was an untidy scrawl as if it had been written in a great hurry.

The message made him sick with fear. He ran a hand over his cropped red hair and looked at the old man who sat opposite him. "Sorry, Professor," the policeman mumbled. "I've got kids of my own. If anything happened to one of them I swear I'd die."

The old man blinked rapidly, impatiently. "Lieutenant Barber, you must forget your personal feelings in this case. You must read that note again . . . and again . . . and again. Until you get inside the mind of the man who wrote it. When we understand him we will catch him. Now, read the note."

Sam swallowed hard and read carefully.

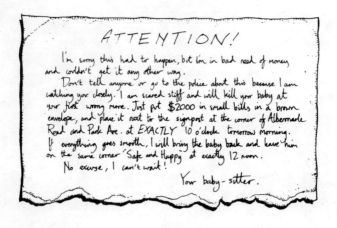

ATTENTION!

I'm sorry this had to happen, but I'm in bad need of money and couldn't get it any other way.

Don't tell anyone or go to the police about this because I am watching you closely. I am scared stiff and will kill your baby at your first wrong move. Just put $2000 in small bills in a brown envelope, and place it next to the signpost at the corner of Albemarle Road and Park Ave. at EXACTLY 10 o'clock tomorrow morning. If everything goes smooth, I will bring the baby back and leave him on the same corner 'Safe and Happy' at exactly 12 noon.

No excuse, I can't wait!

Your baby-sitter.

Professor Elmore nodded slowly. "This was the note found in the pram of baby Peter Weinberger. Now, Lieutenant, you have spoken to Mrs Weinberger. How did she seem to you?"

Sam Barber looked up, puzzled and angry. "Why . . . she was hysterical, of course! How do you think she'd be after her baby's been kidnapped?"

The old man sighed and held up a hand. "Please, answer my questions, Lieutenant. Before we go searching the countryside for kidnappers we must be sure a kidnap has taken place!"

Sam's temper was as fiery as his hair. He opened his mouth to argue angrily . . . then stopped himself. "Sorry, professor. Of course it's a kidnapping! The child is gone – a ransom note is left behind. What's that if it's not a kidnapping?"

The old man simply raised his white eyebrows as if to say, "You tell me."

The detective stared hard at the note in his hand. "You mean . . . it's just possible that Beatrice Weinberger had something to do with the disappearance of her own baby? But why?"

Again the old man waited for the policeman to find the answer to his own question. "Something happened to the kid – it died – she couldn't explain it . . . so she faked the kidnap note to take suspicion away from her?"

"It's possible," the professor said quietly. "So, I repeat my question. How did Mrs Weinberger seem when you spoke to her?"

This time the young policeman thought long and hard before he answered slowly, "Upset . . . very, very upset. No, it wasn't an act. It wasn't!"

"Then who wrote the note?"

"He's got a sick mind, whoever wrote it," Sam said bitterly.

"You're sure it's a man, then?" the professor asked sharply.

Sam closed his eyes and tried to picture him. "Yes. A woman might snatch a kid because she wants a baby. But this kidnapper wants money. It's a man. Am I right? You're the expert on kidnapping, Professor Elmore. What can you tell from the note?"

The old man frowned and leaned forward. "I can tell you that we'll be lucky to get baby Peter back alive," he said gently. "This note is typical of so many I have seen – threatening to harm the victim if the family go to the police; saying that he's 'watching' the family! That's impossible, of course. No, what worries me is the kidnapper admitting he's scared. A scared person can panic. A panicking person could do anything . . . even kill their victim."

Sam nodded heavily. "And the kidnapper is also pretty stupid. He's told us when and where he's going to be to pick up the money."

"And you, Lieutenant? Where will you be?"

"I'll be waiting . . . hidden, of course. We'll arrest him when he shows up . . ."

"But you won't know where the baby's hidden!" the professor objected.

"He'll have to tell us," Sam said.

The old man shook his head sadly. "Lieutenant, you have just one chance. A baby is a noisy, tiring thing to have around you. Especially if you are a frightened man. If you don't get it right first time, then the baby will die."

Sam Barber stuck out his chin. "I'll get it right," he said.

Albermarle Road, 10am, 5 July 1956

Angelo La Marca was sweating until his shirt was soaked. The baby's crying had kept him awake most of the night. Now it was weaker and only gave an occasional whimper.

He sat in the car at the top of Albermarle Road – a quiet road usually, but today there were men around. A road sweeper pushed a broom towards the corner of Park Avenue, but didn't bother collecting the sweepings. Some road-sweeper! La Marca thought, or a cop trying to look like a road sweeper.

Then there was the mail man slowly plodding from house to house. It was late for a mail delivery. And that mail man was looking around him very carefully. Some mail man!

Then a woman in a dark coat hurried to the street corner, looked around nervously and dropped a package by the wall of a house. Clutching a handkerchief to her mouth she practically ran back the way she'd come. He recognised her. Yesterday she'd been pushing a pram. He'd followed her home, scribbled a note as he sat at the wheel of the car and snatched the baby when she went in to find a change of nappy.

Now the parcel with $2000 was waiting for him by the side of the road.

Sweat ran into La Marca's eyes and he brushed it away nervously. The road sweeper had turned and was brushing the gutter he'd just swept clean.

La Marca slipped the car into gear and drove quickly away from the trap. When he reached the main road he braked sharply. The road was deserted. He took the baby in its blanket and placed it in the long grass at the side of the road.

11 July 1956

"He phoned Mrs Weinberger this morning," Sam Barber said.

"The baby will be dead by now," the professor said softly.

"Told her to leave some money in a blue bag she'd find by a mail box," the policeman went on.

"He'll still try for the money . . . even if the victim is dead. And the family will pay up, just in case," the old man said tiredly.

"The bag was attached to a piece of string. The string led into some bushes. He planned to hide in the bushes, wait until the money was in the bag, then pull it towards him. As if we wouldn't notice a blue bag being dragged across the road. He must be stupid!" Sam exploded.

"He is," the professor agreed. "What did he say about the baby?"

Sam took a deep breath. "He said Mrs Weinberger would find it by the side of the Parkway road."

"And did you?"

Sam looked at his chewed fingernails. He'd never bitten his nails before this case began. He shook his head silently.

"Then we must catch the man and bring him to justice," the old man said fiercely.

"We have no clues," the young lieutenant sighed.

"You have the note," the professor reminded him. "Check the handwriting against every known criminal in the country!"

"That'll take forever!" Sam argued.

It took six weeks.

August 1956

La Marca climbed the stairs to his room. It was two in the morning. His wife trailed wearily after him.

From the corner of his eye he saw two shadows waiting at the top of the stairs. He backed away. He signalled to his wife to be silent and began to tiptoe down the way he'd come.

"What's wrong?"

"Police!"

He reached the bottom step and crept into the hallway. The safety of the front door was just a few steps away. Suddenly the hall light snapped on. Police Lieutenant Sam Barber stepped towards La Marca. "What do you want?"

"Mr La Marca?"

"Yes?"

"We were wondering if you could help us with our enquiries."

"Into what?"

"You seem nervous, Mr La Marca."

"You people always make me nervous. Arrested me for making illegal alcohol a couple of years ago."

"This is a matter of a kidnap. The Weinberger baby. Disappeared six weeks ago."

"There's no baby here! Search my flat!"

"Oh, we already have, Mr La Marca . . . we already have! There's no baby there. That doesn't prove you're innocent. You could have dumped him anywhere! We're looking at murder, not kidnapping now."

"And it doesn't prove me guilty either," La Marca sneered.

"You tell him, Angelo!" his wife jeered.

"No. That doesn't prove you're guilty," Sam agreed. "But perhaps this does," he said and held out two pieces of paper. The first was a statement to the police about making illegal alcohol. "Did you write this?" the policeman asked.

"Yes," La Marca said.

"The handwriting is identical to this. So, Mr La Marca . . . did you write this?"

La Marca turned pale as he looked at the scrawled note. "I'm sorry this had to happen, but I'm in bad need of money," it said, "and couldn't get it any other way . . ."

Kidnapping – FACT FILE

The more rich or the more famous you are then the more you are in danger of being kidnapped – or having a relative kidnapped. Some of the most sensational cases have included . . .

1. **The Lindberg Kidnapping.** In 1927 Charles Lindberg was the first man to fly the Atlantic Ocean alone. He won a $25,000 prize and became a hero of the United States – a year later his portrait appeared on a postage stamp. But in 1932 his baby son was kidnapped. A ransom of $50,000 was paid but the baby had died. A German, Richard Hauptmann, was arrested two years later when some of the ransom money was spent by him. He was executed but there are some people who doubt if he was guilty.

2. **The Sinatra Kidnapping.** In 1963 Frankie Sinatra, son of the pop singer Frank, was resting in his hotel room. There was a knock on the door and the call, "Room service!" Frankie opened the door, was seized by a gang and driven off. A ransom of $250,000 was demanded and paid. But, at the drop-off point for the money, Federal Bureau of Investigation (FBI) Officers used infrared cameras to photograph the kidnapper. They also placed an electronic bug in the money case. Once Frankie was released the FBI moved in and arrested three people. Two of them had been at school with Frankie's mother!

3. **The Hearst Kidnapping.** The newspaper millionaire Randolph Hearst had reported the Lindberg kidnap

back in 1932. In 1974 his 19-year-old daughter, Patty, was snatched from her home and a ransom of $3,250,000 was demanded. The kidnappers claimed to be a terrorist group, the Symbionese Liberation Army (SLA). But a curious thing happened to Patty – she found the SLA life more exciting than being a spoilt little rich girl and joined the SLA. She even took part in a bank raid to steal some money for their cause. Patty Hearst was out on another SLA raid when the FBI attacked their headquarters and killed the members in a gun battle. The girl returned in time to see her headquarters in flames. She was arrested for the raids but the court took pity on her and she was given just a short prison sentence.

4. **The Waite Kidnapping.** Terrorist groups in Beirut in the Middle East began kidnapping British, American and French hostages during the 1980s. They wanted special favours for their people and for their friends in jail. They would only discuss their demands with certain trusted people. One person they agreed to talk to was the secretary to the Archbishop of Canterbury, Terry Waite. Waite held several sessions of talks with the kidnappers. Then, finally, he went off to a meeting with them . . . and became a kidnap victim himself. The British government refused to give in to the terrorist demands, so he was held for five years before he was finally released.

5. **The Shergar Kidnapping.** Shergar was one of the best horses ever to race. In 1981 it won the English

Derby and was worth a fortune. Then, one night in 1983, it was kidnapped in Ireland. The kidnappers demanded a ransom of £2,000,000. They never showed up to collect the ransom, however, and the racehorse has never been seen since. Rumours are that it was disguised and raced again under another name in another part of the world. The truth is probably sadder than that.

6.   **The Carolyn Wharton Kidnapping.** At 12.46 p.m. on 19 March 1955, Carolyn Wharton was born in the Baptist hospital of Texas. At 1.15 a woman, disguised as a nurse, walked into the hospital and took Carolyn. So Carolyn made history in being the youngest kidnap victim on record. She was just 29 minutes old.

7.   **The King John Kidnapping.** Kidnapping has not always been seen as a crime. In the Middle Ages the aim of many battles was to kill the poor foot soldiers but to capture the rich knights alive. Then you could hold the knights prisoner until their families paid a fat ransom. Of course you treated the knights very well – after all, next time you might be the one who was taken prisoner! King John II of France was captured at the battle of Poitiers in 1356. He spent three years in the Tower of London with every luxury he wanted while the money was raised to pay his ransom. He had his own cooks and servants and even his own guards!

8.   **The Personal Organiser Kidnapping.** In the 1980s a new type of diary became popular with

businessmen the world over. It was known as a Filofax or a Personal Organiser. The advantage of this type of diary is that you can keep a lot of information in it – all of your important meetings, the phone numbers of your vital business contacts, notes on meetings or ideas you want to keep. Everything. So, if you lost the diary your business life was in chaos – you could lose a fortune by missing important meetings, for example. Gangs of thieves got wise to the value of the Personal Organiser. They began stealing them from pockets and briefcases. They then looked at the address of the owner and offered to return it – for a reward. A very large reward. A ransom in fact.

9.   The greatest kidnapping ransom ever was probably that paid for King Atahualpa of the Incas. The Spanish conquerors of the country demanded that his people fill a hall with the gold and silver of the country. This happened in 1533. It would probably be worth $200,000,000 by today's values. The Spaniards collected the ransom, then killed Atahualpa anyway.

10.   The British police made several mistakes in a 1969 kidnap. It was the first kidnap in modern British history and they had no experience of how to deal with it. They . . .

• received a kidnap note with a criminal's fingerprints on but didn't act because they thought it was a publicity stunt;
• disguised police motorcyclists as Hell's Angels to follow the family to the money dropping place – but

their years of police training gave them away as they
obeyed all the traffic laws and speed limits;

• forgot to tell local police that plain-clothes vehicles
were patrolling the area. The local police tried to
arrest the plain-clothes police for acting suspiciously;

• disguised a burly officer as the daughter of the victim
and sent him on a bus journey to meet up with the
kidnappers. A fellow passenger reported this
peculiar-looking "woman" to the police and again
uniformed officers turned up to arrest the embarrassed, high-heeled detective;

• dropped suitcases of money in a hedge as instructed
by the kidnappers. A local woman found them and
local police came and took them away;

• released details of the kidnap to the press. The
victim's family telephone was jammed with callers
for nine days so the kidnappers couldn't get through.

The victim was never seen again, dead or alive.

DETECTIVES

Blood
on the Floor

The "perfect crime" is one where the clever criminal is never caught. But sometimes the clever criminal comes up against an even cleverer detective. Before Sherlock Holmes was created a young French detective was already showing his brilliance . . .

Paris, France, February 1869

The man was speechless. His wife managed to say, "*Murder?*"

The young detective, Gustave Mace, spoke softly. "I know it must come as a shock. But yes, I have reason to believe that a murder was committed in your room."

"When?" the young man gasped.

"About the middle of last December," the policeman explained. "May we come in? I have two officers here," he went on.

Two burly gendarmes held a smaller, pale young man between them. Gustave Mace explained, "And this is Monsieur Voirbo. He rented this room before you."

Voirbo looked sulky and menacing. He was short but well built and powerful. He played nervously with his black moustache.

The young couple clutched at each other. "The murderer?" the woman breathed.

"That's what we're here to try and prove," the detective said. "May we come in?"

Slowly, unwillingly, the couple led the way into the poor but neat room . . . and suddenly it didn't seem so cosy any more.

"Do you remember how the furniture was arranged when you moved in?" Mace asked.

The woman nodded. "This table was in the centre of the room," she said. The two police guards moved the heavy old table.

"If Bodasse died here then he must have been killed while he was sitting at the table. Voirbo must have cut up the body on the table."

The new owner of the room jumped away from the table as if the body were still there. His wife shrank onto a chair that stood against the wall.

"Sorry, Madame," the detective said quickly. "The details of this crime are too horrible for a lady's ears. But we must face the criminal with the details of his crime."

"Suspect," Voirbo sneered. "I am not a criminal. You can prove nothing, Mace. I am just a suspect and you will have to let me go."

"We shall see," the detective replied. He turned back to the young couple. "Perhaps you would prefer to leave the room."

But the young woman shook her head quickly. "No. I want to know."

The detective gave a nod and sat at the table. "It began in January. A restaurant owner in the Rue Princesse had complaints that his water tasted foul. He had a window in his basement that looked out onto the surface of the water. There were two packages floating there. He fished them out. Each contained the lower part of a leg with a stocking on. The doctors told me they belonged to a man. Then other clues began to turn up. By the end of December two thighs had been found. Then we had a witness who saw something very strange . . . a plump, young man with a moustache was feeding flesh to fish on the river."

All eyes in the room turned to the plump young man with the moustache. Voirbo tried to return their stares with a brave, carefree grin.

"How did you find him?" the young woman asked.

"The killer made one tiny mistake," Mace explained. "He sewed up the body in cloth. But the stitching was superb. It was the work of a tailor! That made our search rather easier."

"And Voirbo is a tailor?" the woman asked.

Mace did not answer directly. "The killer was a tailor who also knew the well in Rue Princesse. Voirbo was a tailor who hired a worker in Rue Princesse."

"That doesn't make me a murderer," Voirbo said with irritation. One of his guards tightened the grip on his arm.

Mace went on, "The body was identified as Bodasse, an old miser. Yet no one had reported Bodasse as being missing. The killer was clever. He had been going to the old man's room for weeks, putting on lights so people would think Bodasse was still alive."

The young woman's eyes brightened. "You put a watch on Bodasse's house?"

Mace nodded. "You would make a good detective, madame."

The young woman blushed. "And Voirbo turned up?"

The detective said, "He did."

"I went to repay some money I'd borrowed," the accused man said.

Mace nodded. "Bodasse's money box was empty. Voirbo paid his rent with the miser's money."

Voirbo looked pleased with himself. "The money I borrowed!"

"We checked this room before you moved in," Mace said to the young woman. "It was clean."

"It was spotless!" the woman agreed.

"*Too* clean!" Mace said eagerly. "We checked with Voirbo's old cleaner. She said that Voirbo was a filthy man. Why did he suddenly become clean? Had he been cleaning something up?"

"The room smelled strongly of cleaning fluid when we moved in," the new tenant remembered.

"I spilled a bottle on the floor. I had to mop it up. I cleaned the rest of the room up while I was about it," Voirbo explained in a tired voice as if bored with the investigation. "A clean room doesn't make me a murderer."

The detective turned sharply to face the accused man. "You have recently married?"

"Yes," Voirbo shrugged.

"We searched your house with the permission of your wife. We found Bodasse's money in a sealed box that was submerged in a cask of wine."

For the first time Voirbo looked uncertain. "The money I borrowed!" He struggled to rise to his feet but the guards held him down on his chair. "You have no proof!"

"Everything points to you," the young woman said. "The tailor who knew the well in Rue Princesse; the man who has Bodasse's fortune hidden away; the man who kept visiting Bodasse's house after his death!"

"Ah! But I can explain everything. I can even tell you who the murderer is!"

The young woman jerked upright in her chair. "You can?"

"It was the butcher called Rifer! Who would cut up his victim? A tailor? No – a butcher!"

The woman looked at Mace. "Do you know Rifer?"

Mace laughed. "We know Rifer. A drunkard and a bully."

"And a murderer!" Voirbo said fiercely.

"Alas, we cannot prove that, can we, Voirbo?"

Voirbo's eyes glittered. "No! The police killed him."

The detective explained calmly to the young couple. "Rifer was arrested for being drunk. He was so violent we had him locked away in an asylum for the insane. He died there."

"He drank himself to death," Voirbo said. "He admitted the murder to me. He drank to forget the horror of the murder."

"He drank because you encouraged him to. He had a weakness for drink. You gave him all the money he needed to drink himself to death," Mace argued.

"He confessed that he killed Bodasse," the accused man said.

"Where did he kill him?"

"In his butcher's shop, of course."

Mace gave a small smile. "So, if I can prove that Bodasse died in this room you will forget this stupid lie about the butcher?"

Voirbo smiled back. The great detective had set the great criminal a challenge. Voirbo was a gambler. This was a gamble for the greatest stake of all – his life. "If you can prove Bodasse died in here then I will admit everything."

Mace nodded slowly and turned to the young woman. "Madame, would you be so kind as to bring me a bowl of water?"

She rose to her feet, took a bowl from the cupboard and hurried to the pump in her yard. A minute later she brought the bowl back, brimming with water, and placed it carefully on the table.

"Now," Mace said, "if Bodasse died here then he was cut up on this table. There would have been a lot of blood . . ."

"But you have not found any blood-stained clothes of mine, have you, Mr Detective?" Voirbo snorted.

"Perhaps you took your clothes off while you did the dreadful deed. Perhaps you burned the clothes?"

Voirbo's lips tightened and he said nothing.

"Now, that blood would flow over the floor. Where would it end up?" the detective asked.

"It would be washed out of the door," the young woman said.

"Ah, but the floor is not perfectly flat! It would gather in pools where the floor dips. It is a stone floor. The blood must have soaked into the cracks between the stones before the rest was washed out of the door. If we pour the water onto the floor then we shall see where it ends up, shall we?"

Voirbo strained against the rough hands of the guards as

Mace carefully tipped the water onto the floor. It formed a pool, then began to trickle towards the door. It settled in a dip in the floor and then began to seep into a crack and disappear.

Mace said, "Do you have a chisel, monsieur?"

The young man nodded and went to bring one. Voirbo had turned pale. Sweat was trickling down his face.

"Is that how it happened?" the detective asked.

Voirbo stayed silent. The young man returned with the chisel. Mace carefully placed the tip into the crack and levered the flat stone up. He turned it over. There was a rust-red stain on the underside.

Voirbo shuddered. His eyes widened with horror. "The old miser's blood!" he croaked.

"You confess?"

"Yes," Voirbo whispered. "I needed ten thousand francs. I was getting married. Her father wouldn't let me marry her unless I had ten thousand francs. I begged Bodasse, I begged him. He didn't need the money! If he'd only let me have the money I wouldn't have had to kill him. Turn it over! Turn the stone over. I thought I'd seen the last of his blood on that floor. I've seen it in my dreams! I never thought I'd really see it again."

He buried his face in his hands until he was hauled to his feet by his guards and dragged off to prison.

The young woman looked at the stone curiously and without fear. "A clever trick, Monsieur Mace . . . but that red stain could be anything. You have no tests to prove that it is blood."

Mace shrugged. "Perhaps not. That is not important. Only one thing matters . . . in the mind of that guilty man it will always be blood."

Detective Work – FACT FILE

1. Voirbo cheated the guillotine. First he attempted to escape but was caught. Then someone smuggled a razor blade into his prison cell. He killed himself before he could be brought to trial and executed. Later, detective work showed that he had probably killed at least three other people before he was arrested for the murder of Bodasse. He had been clever enough to get away with it before – he might have got away with this murder and many others if it hadn't been for the cleverness of the young detective. Nowadays detectives have the help of science.

2. **Blood testing.** At first, blood could only be proved to be human. The first case took place in Berlin in 1904, when Theodore Berger was convicted of murder. Bloodstains in his suitcase were shown to be human. Nowadays bloodstains can be tested and the blood proved to be from one particular human being and no other. A criminal with the blood of a victim on his clothes can no longer say, "I cut myself," or "It's from a slice of meat I bought at the butcher's shop."

3. **Identikit pictures.** These were developed in the 1950s. A Los Angeles detective assembled photographs and cut them up to make a "kit" of jigsaw pieces with 37 noses, 52 chins, 102 pairs of eyes, 40 lips, 130 hairlines and various beards, moustaches, hats, spectacles, wrinkles and eyebrows. In 1959 an armed robber was arrested after his identikit picture was sent around the

district. He was the first of many to be arrested after an identikit release. Nowadays a computer is used to create a picture from the witness's description.

4. **Bullets.** Each gun barrel leaves a mark on its bullets different from that left by any other gun. So, if you find the bullet used in a crime and you find a suspect who owns a gun, you can prove whether or not the bullet came from that gun. This discovery in 1928 led to the arrest of two men in England who had shot a policeman.

5. **Fingerprints.** The first police force to adopt the use of fingerprints for fighting crime was that of Buenos Aires. A woman claimed her neighbour had killed her children. He was beaten up but refused to confess. Inspector Alvarez found bloodstained fingerprints on the doorpost of the house. They were those of the mother, not the neighbour. She was sentenced to life imprisonment. Nowadays all criminals know about fingerprints, so they usually wear gloves. In 1978 Canadian scientists were able to identify ten-year-old fingerprints using the latest laser technology.

6. **Bugging.** Detectives can use tape-recorders the size of a cigarette packet which will fit in the pocket yet pick up conversations across the room. They can also listen to criminals' telephone conversations using special radio receivers.

7. **Chemical testing.** Arsenic poison was a popular murder weapon in the early years of the nineteenth century. The victim died with violent stomach pains, but doctors had to admit that it could be a natural stomach fever. Then, in 1836, James Marsh found a test which could prove that the victim had suffered from arsenic poisoning. Nowadays there are tests for every poison known. Only in murder mystery stories do you find the untraceable poison.

8. **Lie detectors.** In 1902 a Scottish doctor invented a machine which measured pulse rates and helped to show when a suspect was lying.

9. **Radio.** Radio messages travel faster than any criminal can. Police can have details of the crime and criminal sent to every corner of the world in minutes. The first criminal to be caught using radio was Doctor Hawley Harvey Crippen. In 1910 Crippen murdered his wife and sailed for Canada with his lover on the SS *Montrose*. Captain Kendall of the *Montrose* picked up the "wanted" message, recognised the Doctor and radioed back that he was on board. Inspector Dew of Scotland Yard took a faster ship and reached Canada before Crippen. He climbed on board the *Montrose* as

it approached Quebec. "Good morning, Doctor Crippen," he said. Crippen shuddered. The shock struck him dumb for a moment, then he murmured, "Thank God it's over. The suspense has been too great. I couldn't stand it any longer."

10.   **Police cars.** The first in the world was a Stanley Steamer brought by Boston Police in the USA. But four years earlier a policeman in Northampton, England, had borrowed a Benz car to chase a man who was selling forged circus tickets. The man, who tried to run away, was caught! Perhaps a police dog would have been useful – the first official police dog was a bull terrier used by Scottish police to catch whisky

smugglers in 1816. It was taught to grab suspects' horses by the nose so as to make them rear up and drop their illegal loads. It worked! But the smugglers took their revenge and shot the dog six months later.

If science has helped the police then it has also helped the criminal. Vast sums of money are stolen every year through computer fraud. Cars break shop windows better than a brick and the police are now faced with the "ram raid". Today's cars can cost more than a house but are easier to steal and take away!

HIJaCKeRS
The
First Hijack

One twentieth-century invention gave criminals a completely new set of crimes to invent. The aeroplane . . .

The Pacific Ocean, 16 July 1947

The Catalina Flying Boat lifted from the waters of Macao and dragged its bulk into the clear Pacific air. The water below shimmered and Wong Yu couldn't take his eyes away from it.

"Beautiful," he breathed.

"But when do we attack?" Tok asked, nudging Wong.

"Not yet, not yet! Relax. Enjoy the flight. Enjoy the view!"

"I can't *see* the view," Tok grumbled. "You have the seat by the window."

"Quite rightly," his partner said. "This is my plan. When we are rich you can buy an aircraft of your own and look out of every window!"

"You are sure the plan will work?" Tok whispered and felt the warm, heavy pistol under his cotton jacket.

"My plans always work. This one is my *best* plan. No one has *ever* thought of this before! It is brilliant!"

"What if they don't do as they are told?"

"I have a gun. You have a gun. If you did *not* have a gun and I pointed my gun at you, what would you do?" Wong asked patiently.

"Run away!" Tok said quickly.

Wong took his eyes away from the window. He frowned at Tok. Perhaps the man was stupid. Perhaps he shouldn't have brought him. He'd go through it again. "We are on an aeroplane. There is nowhere to run to, Tok. We wait half an hour. When I give the signal, you walk forward to that door at the front of the plane . . ."

"The nose!"

"What about it?"

"That's what they call the front of the plane. The nose. I read it in a book!"

"You read a book? Well done, Tok. You must be cleverer than you look."

"Thank you, Wong Yu."

"You ask to see the driver . . ."

"Pilot, Wong Yu."

"All right, pilot. You take out your gun and point it at his head. You say, *Take this plane to Pearl River*. The pilot will fly to Pearl River. He will land on the river. The plane is full of English and Americans. They are rich. We will hold them at gunpoint. We will send letters to their friends asking for lots and lots of money . . ."

"I cannot write in English," Tok reminded his partner.

"We will tell our prisoners to write to their families, all right? Now, when the money arrives we set them free."

"And if the money doesn't arrive?"

"We shoot them."

"And the plane?"

"We sell that too. We will have riches beyond dreams, Tok – riches beyond dreams."

Wong Yu closed his eyes and listened to the drone of the huge engines. He felt the aircraft tremble as it climbed above the clouds.

When he opened his eyes again and looked out of the window he was surprised to see the coast. Perhaps he had fallen asleep for a while. It was time for action.

Wong nodded to Tok. Tok's eyes were wide and staring. He rose from his seat like a machine and marched to the cabin door. He tapped politely on the door and listened for an invitation to enter. The noise of the plane must have drowned the knocking. Wong rolled his eyes and waved a hand for Tok to go in.

The man took out his gun and entered the cabin.

Wong leaned forward in his seat. Tok had been gone ten seconds now – the plane would change direction at any moment. Twenty seconds. Wong heard a cry. He jumped to his feet and moved towards the front. Tok crashed into him as he staggered out of the cabin clutching his blood-soaked head, then fell to the floor groaning.

Wong stepped over his partner and saw the co-pilot advancing. He was a large Scotsman with a fierce red face, and he was waving an iron bar. He raised the bar and was about to crunch it onto Tok's skull again when Wong pulled out the gun.

The plane began to turn. Wong overbalanced and his shot missed the Scotsman. As the plane steadied he tried again. The co-pilot ducked back into the cabin just as Wong fired a second shot. The bullet scorched past him and struck the pilot in the back.

The man fell forward and the weight of his body pushed the control stick forward. The roar of the engines grew louder as the plane tipped into a dive. The co-pilot hesitated. He wanted to chase Wong and thrash him with the iron bar but he knew he had to try and save the plane. He threw down the bar and struggled to move his pilot from the controls.

Wong backed along the aisle. Passengers had begun screaming and struggling in their seat belts in panic. Wong kept going towards the back of the plane. The craft was spinning wildly now and Wong felt as if the world was turning upside down.

At last he reached the little room at the back of the plane, grabbed hold of the door frame, pulled himself through and slammed the door.

He pressed his back to the wall and felt it tremble as if it was being dragged across a field of boulders. There were tremendous cracking noises as parts of the airframe snapped under the strain. "Ah! It was such a good idea!" Wong cried as the force of gravity from the spin made him black out.

He was unconscious when the plane hit the water.

"Such a good idea," he murmured.

"What was that?" an American voice asked.

Wong opened his eyes. His head hurt. He felt as if every rib had been snapped. A clear white light shone on his face. The smell of antiseptic filled his broken nose.

"Where . . . am I alive?"

"Speak English, pal?" the American said.

Wong felt the cool pillow under his head. Carefully, slowly, he turned his head to where the voice came from. It took him a while to focus. He was in bed. A hospital bed. The man with the American voice lay next to him.

"Hi!" the American said. He had cropped grey hair and a face as hard as sandstone. "You feel OK?"

"OK?"

"Yeah, all right?"

"Yes, thank you – all right."

"Guess you're the luckiest man alive," the American said.

"Nearly killed! How am I lucky?" Wong asked.

"Because all the rest *were* killed. You're the only survivor."

"Survivor?"

"Only one left."

Wong closed his eyes. Poor Tok. Still, it was all Tok's fault. He'd allowed that man to attack him. It was such a good idea! Wong fell asleep.

When he woke next time he was able to sit up and eat. After two days he was sore and stiff but alert as ever.

The American in the next bed was friendly, and he was cleverer than Tok. Wong still knew it had been a good idea! Next time he'd get it right.

"Do you want to make money?" he asked the American one afternoon.

The grey-haired man shrugged. "Doesn't everyone?"

"I have an idea . . . such a good idea," Wong said proudly.

"An idea for making money?" the American said.

"Much, much money. Enough to last you two lifetimes," Wong promised.

"Legal?"

"Ah, no," Wong said. "You are perhaps interested in crime?"

The stone-faced man leaned forward. "That's my business!"

"A criminal?"

"I know *hundreds* of them. What's this plan?"

And Wong told him.

When he'd finished the American pressed the bell that would summon a nurse. "And was this the stunt you were trying to pull when your plane crashed?"

"Don't worry! Don't worry! It won't happen next time! Next time it will be perfect."

The nurse stuck her head around the door. "You rang, Inspector Bacchus?"

Wong Yu looked puzzled. "Inspector? Please, what is inspector? I thought your name was Joe?"

The policeman ignored the Chinese hijacker and spoke to the nurse, his voice cold as steel.

"Tell the local police to arrest this man."

The nurse wasn't sure whether or not this was a joke. But the expression on the inspector's face convinced her it wasn't. "What's the charge?"

"The charge is murder."

Within two weeks, Wong Yu had signed a confession. "Such a good idea," he sighed as he was led to his execution.

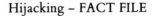

Hijacking – FACT FILE

1. The term hijack probably comes from the phrase used by the robbers who took over vehicles stopped on the highways of the United States in the 1930s. The robber would stop a loaded truck, pull out a gun, point it at the driver and say, "Stick 'em up, *high, Jack!*"

2. In 1976 the world's worst hijacker struck. He was on a flight across the United States when he jumped up from his seat and pointed a gun at the stewardess. "Take me to Detroit!" he cried.

"But sir," the stewardess explained as calmly as she could, "we are already going to Detroit."

"Are we? Ah . . . that's all right then," he muttered and sat down again.

3. An equally stupid hijacker boarded an Arab airliner in 1967. He threatened the captain and insisted that the plane go to Jerusalem. "But sir," the Captain said, "the Arabs are at war with Israel. You are an Arab. If we take you to Jerusalem you will be shot as soon as you step off the plane!"

The captain said later that the man was drunk and had to be protected from himself.

4. The largest hijack ransom ever paid was $6 million. The Japanese government paid this in exchange for an aircraft with 38 hostages on board held at Dacca Airport, Bangladesh.

5.   Skyjacking is becoming rarer now. Airlines have X-ray checks on passengers and luggage, so it's extremely difficult to take a weapon on board. And most governments refuse to pay a ransom. It was easier in the 1960s when an unknown man held an aeroplane and its passengers hostage on the runway. He demanded $300,000 . . . and a parachute. He got both and then ordered the plane to take off. By the time it had landed the man was gone. He'd parachuted to freedom somewhere over the Mid-West and was never traced.

GANGSTERS
The
Tatooed Arm

*Professional gangsters think of absolutely everything to avoid being caught
. . . they can allow for everything except simple bad luck!*

Sydney, Australia – April, 1935

"Roll up! Roll up! See the monstrous Tiger Shark!" the
showman cried. Families were flocking to Hobson's Aquarium
on Coogee Beach near Sydney. It was a beautiful Australian
autumn day – a day for swimming and sunbathing and
sandcastles under a brilliant blue sky. Hardly a day for thoughts
of murder.

"Take me to see the shark, Daddy!" little Pete Chapman
cried.

His father shrugged. Why not? Detective Sergeant Chapman
didn't spend enough time with his son. The Sydney police
department kept him much too busy.

Sergeant Chapman paid and took Pete's hand and led him
round the rows of tanks with fish of every size and colour and
shape. Little Pete dragged at his father's arm. "The shark,
Daddy! Which one's the shark?"

The policeman nodded to where the greatest crowd had
gathered in front of a large new tank with glass sides and a
silver-grey shadow sliding around inside.

"I can't see, Daddy!" the boy whispered. Somehow the
shadow of the shark had cast a cloak of silence over the
watchers.

The crowd was moving slowly past the new tank. Sergeant
Chapman and Pete joined the queue. An old man leaned against
a rail and grinned at them. His hair was coarse and grey and his
unshaven face weathered to a rusty brown. "Like my shark,
son?"

"*Your* shark?"

"Sure," the old man nodded. "Caught him three weeks ago.

My brother owns this aquarium so we brought him in alive. Fourteen feet long!" The old man added slyly, "A shark inside a shark!"

Little Pete's mouth fell open. "A shark inside a shark?"

"That's right. Caught a small shark and started to reel him onto the boat. Along came this feller and swallowed the little one. It took three of us to haul them all on board." The old man bent forward and said quietly, "Want a real close look?"

Pete nodded dumbly. The old man winked at Sergeant Chapman. "Come round to the back . . . a private view!"

He led the way through piles of timber that smelled of salt and fish and into the dark, cool centre of the square of tanks. The tiger shark twitched its tail angrily and fixed Pete with glittering black eyes. The boy's mouth went dry and he stepped back. The two men chatted quietly about fishing while Pete crept closer again. Suddenly he gasped, "Hey! Dad! The shark's being sick!"

They watched as the tiger shark opened its razor-lined mouth and spewed out a mess of foul old food. "Sharks often do that," the old man explained. "Clears their stomachs."

Then the creature shuddered with one last effort and something large and loathsome slid out. Sergeant Chapman pulled his son away. "Clear the aquarium," he said sharply. "I'm a police officer and I'm ordering you to close immediately!"

The old man peered into the murky water. "What is it?"

Sergeant Chapman held his trembling son and mouthed the words over the boy's head. "An arm. A human arm!"

Sergeant Chapman looked at the frightened, sweating man in the prison cell. "There was a knotted rope around the wrist of the arm in the shark. There was a tattoo of two boxers on the forearm. We checked the fingerprints too. The arm belonged to an amateur boxer called James Smith. He worked in Sydney as a boat-builder. James Smith worked for you, didn't he, Mr Holmes?"

Reg Holmes licked the sweat off his lip and croaked, "Yes."

"James Smith was friendly with a forger called Patrick Brady – do you know Patrick Brady?"

Reg Holmes ran a hand over his greasy hair, then shook his head.

"No!"

"The dead man was sharing a cottage with Patrick Brady. Brady knows you, Reg!"

"No!" the fat little man squeaked.

"Brady says you were part of the forgery racket," the policeman insisted.

"No!"

"We think Patrick Brady murdered James Smith. We think you know that, Reg. Why don't you tell us? What are you scared of?" Sergeant Chapman said gently.

Reg Holmes took a grubby handkerchief from his pocket and wiped his sweating brow. "He'd kill me too!" he groaned.

The policeman smiled. "So, Patrick Brady *did* kill James Smith, yes?"

"Yes."

"There was an old tin trunk in their cottage, the owner says. Now there's a new tin trunk. We guess that Patrick Brady murdered James Smith and put the body in the trunk." Sergeant Chapman leaned forward. "Why did he cut off the arm, Reg?"

Reg Holmes' little eyes went wide. "The shark! The shark chewed it off!"

The policeman shook his head. "No, our experts say the cut was a clean one. Somebody did it with a knife before the body was dumped in the sea. We guess that the arm wouldn't fit so Patrick Brady cut it off, tied it to the outside of the trunk and dumped it out at sea. He almost got away with it! We'd never have known about the murder because we'd never have found the rest of the body. It was just a freak of fate that the shark swallowed the arm and then ended up in the Hobson Aquarium. A million to one chance. We've arrested Brady. We just needed you to tell the court what you know, Reg."

"He'll kill me!" the little man moaned again.

"He's safely locked away in our cells, Reg."

"He has friends," Reg Holmes breathed. "Friends mixed up with drug smuggling and things. They've killed before. They'll kill me to keep me quiet!"

"We'd look after you. Just sign this statement, then you can go home," the policeman said, pushing a pen towards the frightened man.

Reg Holmes signed. He was signing his own death warrant.

Sergeant Chapman's footsteps echoed down the corridors of the prison as he marched towards Patrick Brady's cell. The doors rattled open then crashed shut behind him. "Now, Mr Brady, why don't you just confess?"

The forger looked up slyly. "Confess to what, sergeant?"

"To the murder of your partner, James Smith."

"Is he dead?" Patrick Brady asked cunningly.

"We've identified the arm . . ." the policeman began.

"My lawyer says an arm is not a body. You can't charge me with murder without a body!" the criminal crowed.

"We have the arm . . ." the sergeant said patiently.

"But James Smith could be wandering around without it," Patrick Brady shrugged. "You know that! Your judges know that. That's why you can't do a thing unless I confess. Am I right?"

"You killed him in the cottage that you shared at Cronulla. You cut up the body on a mattress and put it in the trunk."

"Find any blood in the cottage?" the killer asked impudently. The policeman stayed silent. "And what did I do with the mattress?"

"Threw it in the sea with the trunk."

"And you haven't found either. Think what you like, you can't prove a thing."

"We have a witness," Sergeant Chapman said carefully. "Someone who heard you boast about killing James Smith."

Patrick Brady showed yellowing teeth in a wide grin. "Little Reg Holmes? I don't think little Reg will be giving evidence against anyone."

"We'll see," the policeman snapped and marched back to the police office.

The desk officer looked up as Sergeant Chapman stalked in. "Message for you, Sarge. Just came through. A suspect in that forgery case has just been found dead in his car near Sydney fishing quay. Shot three times with a .32 revolver."

Sergeant Chapman sank into the chair and buried his face in his hands. "And I suppose you're going to tell me his name was Reg Holmes?"

"Yes, Sarge. How did you know?"

Little Pete Chapman made one last visit to the tiger shark before the aquarium closed for the winter.

"Did you catch the man that cut off the tattooed arm, Dad?"

His father watched wearily as the shark swept around the tank. "We caught him."

"Will they hang him?"

"No, Pete, they won't hang him. He'll go to prison for forgery . . . but he got away with the murder charge. We didn't have a body . . . and our only witness died."

"That's bad luck," Pete said.

Sergeant Chapman shook his head. "That's not what police

work is all about, Pete. When that shark was caught, and that arm appeared, we had the most amazing luck in the history of crime. And we still lost the case. Don't talk to me about luck!"

The Law of Chance – FACT FILE

With so many millions of crimes being committed there are bound to be curious twists of fate that turn the best-laid plans of criminals into disaster.

1.   In 1975 a gang of three set out to rob the Royal Bank of Scotland. As they entered the building the revolving doors jammed and they had to be helped out by staff. They thanked the staff and left. The gang returned a few minutes later and demanded £5000. The staff who'd seen the farce of the revolving door thought this was just another joke and laughed at the gang. The leader cut his demand to £500, then 50p. Still the staff couldn't take them seriously. So one of the gang jumped over the counter, but sprained his ankle. The other two dashed for the exit – and became stuck in the revolving door.

2.   In 1979 a Barnsley man set off to do some shoplifting in a large store. As he snatched an item he was grabbed by half a dozen store detectives. He had picked a day when all the store detectives of the district were having a training session – in the store he chose to rob.

3.   A British politician, Horatio Bottomley, was a fairly successful fraudster. One of his greatest schemes came to a disastrous end. He bought six horses and entered them for a race in Belgium. He instructed the six jockeys on exactly which order he wanted them to

finish. He then placed large bets with bookmakers on the exact finishing order. Unfortunately the race course was beside the sea and it was common for sea mists to seep in and cover it. That day the fog was so thick the jockeys lost contact in the fog. They came across the finish line in the wrong order and Bottomley lost a fortune.

4.   In 1976 two men in Blackburn tried to sell a car they had stolen earlier. They were arrested. The man they tried to sell the car to knew it was a stolen vehicle – he was the owner!

5.   In 1977 a man was knocked down by a car in New York. He jumped to his feet with only a couple of bruises. "Lie down!" a passer-by advised him. "If you act really hurt then the insurance company could pay you a fortune." The victim lay down in front of the car and put on a great act of suffering to try and cheat the insurance. Then the car rolled forward and crushed him.

6.   During a smash–and–grab raid in Zurich the thief's finger was sliced off by the glass of the broken window. Police checked the print on the fingertip left behind and arrested the thief.

7.   A Danish bank robber rushed out into the street with his loot and flagged down a taxi. He told the driver to take him to his home address. But the light on top of the car was not a taxi sign – it was a police car.

This man was only slightly luckier than the San Fernando bank robber who dashed into the road clutching a small fortune and was run over by his own getaway driver.

8.   In 1986 an unlucky English hold-up robber wrote a note saying, "*I have a gun in my pocket. Hand over the money or I will shoot.*" At the first shop, a chemist's, the girl behind the counter refused to read the note because she thought it was a rude message. At the next shop the owner was Asian and said, "Sorry, I don't read English." At the Chinese take-away the manager also apologised that he couldn't read the note. "Sorry. I don't have my glasses with me!" He said he'd go and look for them in the back of the shop. In fact, he phoned the police who arrested the young robber.

9.   In Norwich in 1975 a couple went to a dog show with their Afghan hound. The dog disgraced itself and made a mess on the grass. To save anyone trampling in it, the owner scooped up the dog's droppings, wrapped it in newspaper and placed the package in a plastic carrier bag. There was no waste bin nearby so the owners placed the bag in the boot of the car and went off to the show ring. When they returned the boot of the car had been opened. A thief had run off with the only thing in the boot, hoping to open that carrier bag and find a valuable treasure . . .

10.   Not all criminals fail through bad luck. Some are simply stupid. A shop raider in California disguised

himself with a hood made from a pillowcase. This led to his downfall. He stumbled around the store, crashing into counters because he hadn't had the sense to cut eye holes in the material! When he lifted the pillowcase to find the exit, he was recognised by a customer and later arrested. Was he any worse off than Eddie McAlea, who threatened a jeweller with a fake gun? The jeweller didn't move. Eddie had forgotten to take the cork out of the barrel of his pop-gun. He was jailed for six years.

John was a quiet boy. Not very bright at school, but he never made trouble.

He had caring parents and a loving girlfriend, Susan. John didn't have a job or much chance of getting one when he left school. Still, John was healthy and his life was comfortable.

John was sixteen years old.

John was a criminal.

Late one night, when he'd said goodnight to Susan, he met a school friend on the corner of a dark and lampless street.

They didn't speak. They didn't need to. They knew what they were going to do.

In the silent lane behind the houses they found the car. It was the finest and fastest in the village. John's friend broke the locks with amazing speed and within a minute John was behind the wheel.

Five minutes later he waited with the engine rumbling as his friend pulled alongside him in a second stolen car. He gave John a signal. Tyres screamed and engines shattered the peace of the midnight air as they set off to race around the country lanes.

At first John drove as fast as his skill allowed him. He'd always loved cars. His friends had taught him to drive stolen cars on hidden roads and he'd learned quickly. Now, tonight, he was on his own. Sometimes the power of the car seemed to give it a life of its own. His friend had been driving longer and he pulled clear. John was alone on the lonely road and getting nearer and nearer the limit of his skill.

The road unwound in the headlights like the screen of some computer game. But a flash of blue in the mirror caught John's eye.

A police car was following.

Now John pushed his right foot down on the accelerator. The car jumped faster. The corners came more quickly and were gone in a cloud of smoking rubber. The blue light disappeared.

John thought he'd lost the police. In fact they'd slowed down, unwilling to get involved in a dangerous chase.

But John couldn't slow down. In his mind they were on his tail. They were the enemy and they brought shame and disgrace with them. Shame for Susan and his parents. Disgrace with his thieving friends – for the greatest crime was being caught.

The car was good but it couldn't take the corner at that speed. It began to slide. John hadn't the experience to know how to handle it. He twisted the steering further and tried to brake. That was the worst possible thing to do.

The car shot off the road, skidded over the grass verge and headed towards a field.

Perhaps John was unlucky. Perhaps he didn't deserve any luck. But instead of smashing through the fence and coming to a harmless halt in the muddy field he hit an electricity pole. The pole snapped in two and crashed onto the car roof. Live electric cables snaked down and sparked against the twisted car.

John was a quiet boy.

John was a criminal.

John was dead.

Some people commit crime because it's exciting. Perhaps John did. We'll never know, will we?

Crime can be exciting, but usually the rewards are not worth the risks.

But there is one way we can enjoy all the thrill of crime without any of the shame and disgrace of being caught.

We can read about it! Some of the world's oldest stories are crime stories. We can share the dangers, the horrors and the battles of wits between the lawful and the lawless.

Most of those stories are fiction written for adults. This book is written for young people – and every story here is true. As true as the story of John.

John wasn't a very good reader. That's a pity. If he had been, then he might have found safer thrills in books such as this. Millions of others around the world do.

This book is not written for John and the others like him. It is written for John's victims – for his grieving parents, for Susan who still has to live with her pain, and for John's teachers who still wonder where they went wrong. I know, because I was one of those teachers.

TRUE MONSTER STORIES

Incredible? Impossible? Too awful to imagine? But someone, somewhere, at some time has sworn that each of these strange stories is true . . .

A newspaper reports of a monster man, whose fiery breath scorched the faces of his victims.

An American swears to his dying day, he was kidnapped by a family of Bigfoot or ape men.

And centuries old records tell of a beached sea monster so huge, a man could be drowned inside it.

Read accounts of the Yeti, the vampire, and less well-known beasts, like Black Dog and Morgawr; consider the facts and decide for yourself whether these monster stories really are true. And even if you choose not to believe, beware! These tales may linger in your thoughts and darken your dreams . . .

TRUE
HORROR
STORIES

Incredible? Impossible? Too awful to imagine? But someone, somewhere, at some time has sworn that each of these strange stories is true . . .

A girl murders her own father and mother in cold blood.

A whole village of people disappears without trace, and all anyone saw were strange lights in the sky.

An Egyptian mummy, disturbed after thousands of years, leaves a trail of horrible disasters.

Some of these stories have possible explanations, but for others there is *no* answer. Consider the facts and decide for yourself whether each gruesome story really is true – but keep the cover firmly closed once darkness falls, or your dreams could turn into NIGHTMARES . . .